PURCHASING MANAGER'S DECISION HANDBOOK

Purchasing Manager's Decision

HANDBOOK

by DENNIS A. KUDRNA

CAHNERS BOOKS

A Division of Cahners Publishing Company, Inc.
89 Franklin Street, Boston, Massachusetts 02110

Second Printing

Library of Congress Cataloging in Publication Data

Kudrna, Dennis A   1945-
  Purchasing manager's decision handbook.

  Includes index.
  1. Purchasing. I. Title.
HF5437.K82   658.7'2   74-23120
ISBN 0-8436-1307-6

Library of Congress Catalog Card Number: 74-23120
ISBN: 0-8436-1307-6

Printed in the United States of America

Contents

Foreword

Unquestionably, this book makes a distinct contribution to purchasing literature and is in step with contemporary forward-looking management thinking. To best assess this work, one needs to give thought to decision theory analysis, its scope and promise, for the author, Mr. Kudrna, has produced for the purchasing profession an adaptation of the systematic decision theory approach to the field of buying; and he has done it with an instinct and knowledge for the buying game itself that no theoretician could provide. In this respect, this book is an impressive work. It is directed primarily to the buyer who aspires to be truly professional.

Decision theory analysis (DTA) is a modern problem-solving systems approach; the author has focused specifically on purchasing and materials. DTA first stipulates the decision alternatives open to the buyer, second, gets the buyer to make a probabilistic statement as to this assessment of critical uncertainties involved in a buying decision, and third, requires that he quantify or place value on possible results if various actions are taken. This is a logic-oriented framework and the book takes the buyer step-by-step through specific purchasing procedures, such as make-or-buy analysis. Specific instructions are presented explaining how and where to get certain data and in what sequence this information will be required in order to come to a logical conclusion.

It should be emphasized that this is a very down-to-earth book. One must be theoretical first before becoming practical. This book follows a basic theory, yet it is very practically written in a step-by-step manner. Through reference to the *Purchasing Manager's Decision Handbook,* buying techniques can be picked up by one who may have never been faced with a certain purchasing decision because he can be led down the path to think through to a logical conclusion.

Examples of the practical applicable techniques are: simplified tables to show when cash discounts should be taken, the penalty of progress payments, and an analysis of hidden costs resulting from early shipment. A strength the book provides is in depicting specific forms and data, indicating where information must be sought and what needs to be done and then explaining what to do next. In that sense, this book might have been termed "The Professional Buyer's Complete Handbook." This book is directed toward inexperienced or newer buyers as well as those seeking more effective results.

Decision theory advocates assert that this technique will be to the businessman in the future what slide rules and math tables are to the engineer today. Some advocates believe the businessman in the distant future will not be able to cope with complex business problems without a formalized, systematized, and mathematical approach.

Definite advantages of using the DTA approach as exemplified in the *Purchasing Manager's Decision Handbook* are: (1) it causes a focus on critical elements of a buying decision (2) it brings into focus the hidden assumptions behind the decision and shows the logic involved, (3) it provides a means of communicating the reasoning behind a recommended decision or course of action.

Critics of the DTA approach who have a "show me" attitude maintain that a real obstacle is in personal competence and a scarcity of trained practitioners who have the orientation to apply decision theory in the business climate. True, many successful buyers today don't understand DTA or use it, so some could conclude that you don't need to bother with it. Further, some buyers will feel a distinct discomfort about this book as they find themselves trying to think in terms of an unfamiliar mold — *a new approach to better buying*. Yet, to those who aspire to greater effectiveness in achieving lowest-cost buying decisions and improvement, this book will be a refreshing experience. As a handbook it is available for reference when it is timely to refresh the subject and to act. Success to be derived from using this work depends upon how eager the buyers and their managers are to improve the quality of their decision-making process through study and acceptance of a proven systematic approach now applied for the first time to the buying job itself. The would-be professional will find this book of considerable interest at minimum and of much help to him in applying his talents to the creative side of the buying job.

VICTOR H. POOLER
Director of Purchasing
Carrier Division, Carrier Corporation
Syracuse, New York

⹀Preface

The *Purchasing Manager's Decision Handbook* was written to lay a foundation for effective purchasing decisionmaking. In order to accomplish this, it provides a framework for purchasing that will lead inexperienced or inefficient buyers to the best decisions and will allow effective, experienced buyers to support their intuitive judgments with facts. It delineates purchasing decisions, identifies the information necessary for effective decisionmaking, and describes how to efficiently collect and apply this information to identify a decision-making situation, determine the best course of action and establish a target for negotiation.

The presentation of this framework complements two outstanding purchasing personality traits: pragmatism and cynicism. Since the purchasing man is a pragmatist, the body of the book does not include mathematical justification of the concepts proposed but does include detailed application procedures. As a result of this organization, the reader can quickly and easily identify those concepts of value prior to wading through complex supporting formulations. Further, he can realize this value simply by extracting and implementing the accompanying procedures.

Since the purchaser is also a cynic, detailed justification is provided in the Appendixes. Consequently, the reader is able to review the justification himself or, if time does not permit, transfer this task to another for assurance that this framework will provide the results described.

This book has not been written to serve as an introduction to purchasing. There are many excellent books available on that subject which identify and define purchasing considerations and the associated jargon. *Purchasing Manager's Decision Handbook* starts where these "primers" leave off by showing how to effectively apply these considerations. The following example illustrates the difference between the two approaches and the need in purchasing for this decision-making structure. It is concerned with just one of many purchasing decisions: vendor selection. Most, and possibly all, of the existing purchasing books discuss vendor selection by reviewing and defining considerations such as price, terms of payment, assurance of supply, quality, freight, warranty, etc., and showing how each of these considerations contributes to cost and affects vendor selection. However, they do not explain how a purchaser can quantify and apply these considerations in order to reach an effective decision in a case where no one vendor is the lowest in all of these costs.

As an example of the problem that this omission causes, I turn for a moment to my own experience. When I took my first position in purchasing, I was told that all buyers were to insure lowest net applied cost, supply, and sufficient quality to meet the application. I tried to find out how to consider all of these factors simultaneously, but no matter what book I read or to whom I talked, I could not learn how to weigh price against quality and supply. The suggestions I received ranged from "Every situation is unique. There is no one answer," to "You must assure quality and supply at any cost," to "You will learn through experience."

The first answer, that every situation is unique, may have been true but was no help at all. I still had to make decisions and had no guidance. The second suggestion, to assure quality and supply at any cost, was worse because it provided misdirection, not just lack of direction. It is often less costly to accept the inefficiency resulting from late delivery and insufficient quality than to pay the price to assure performance in these factors. The third answer, that one learns through experience, not only leaves the new buyer in the lurch, but also, in many cases, holds forth false promise. Experience is an excellent instructor but learning solely through experience can be costly when it means making mistakes, and it provides no guarantee of developing correct habits since this type of learning is unstructured and entirely dependent on multiple exposure to specific situations.

To function effectively at that point, I did not need a promise that all would work out in the end. I needed a decision-making structure that could guide me to the best decision available even though I lacked experience. Once I had gained experience, I still had need for the same structure, not necessarily to assure that the best possible decisions were made, but to allow me to check and justify those decisions based on my intuitive judgment of commodities.

This book provides the needed structure by using information currently available in your department to quantify costs other than price, much as the experienced buyer does intuitively. Also, it offers procedures to assure that these quantifications, when applied, will result in good decisions. With this structure you will be able to supplement the knowledge of the inexperienced buyer and complement the "gut feel" of the effective buyer to assure that your material dollar is spent wisely.

PURCHASING MANAGER'S DECISION HANDBOOK

=1

Overview of Decision Application

As a result of the computer age and its accompanying information explosion, more information is available than ever before to aid in making purchasing decisions. You can now obtain practically any information you require.

The availability of information, however, does not in itself guarantee efficiency. Having too much information and being unable to differentiate between the useful and the not useful can be as great a roadblock to effective decisionmaking as not having enough information.

Consequently, it is necessary to identify the types of purchasing decisions that must be made and to answer the following questions concerning information requirements:

1. What information do I need?
2. In what form do I need it?
3. How do I use it?

The effective purchasing manager has resolved these questions to his own satisfaction. Unfortunately, operating priorities often prevent formalization of these resolutions, leaving buyers to trial-and-error experimentation to derive their own solutions.

The objective of this presentation is to begin the formal identification of information systems necessary for effective decisionmaking and to describe a method of information application that will allow optimal use of a buyer's time and the best yield.

1

PURCHASING OBJECTIVES

Since an information system will have no value in purchasing unless it aids in decisionmaking, it is necessary to first identify the decisions that must be made and then tailor information requirements to them. This process must be initiated by a statement and analysis of purchasing objectives.

If our goal can be defined as obtaining maximum value on the purchase of services and commodities, purchasing must, to reach this goal, obtain the lowest total of material-related costs and purchasing administrative costs. However, in making decisions to obtain this lowest total, one cannot consider these two costs to be independent and equal in priority. Material-related costs must be the dominant consideration with administrative decisions being determined by material-cost outcomes. The reason behind this approach becomes clearer when you consider management's purpose in creating a Purchasing Department. Management has defined this function, separate from others, in an effort to control and optimize the company's investment in materials. Therefore, by organizational charter, all purchasing decisions must revolve around the consideration of material costs. In this light, the approach to administrative cost is dependent on material-cost efficiency and becomes one of staffing only to that point at which investment in an additional person will not yield benefits in material-cost minimization sufficient to justify the expense.

In accordance with the above, necessary purchasing decisions can be grouped into two categories: material-related cost decisions and decisions concerning the value of administrative cost changes with respect to material-related cost. It is these decisions that purchasing information and decision systems must serve.

Material-Related Cost Minimization

The material-related cost areas influenced by the typical purchasing activities of vendor selection, relay of vendor technological developments, negotiation, expediting, and development of alternate procurement practices may be depicted as follows:

1. Net price
2. Transportation cost
3. Inventory expense
4. Quality cost
5. Design cost
6. Manufacturing cost

Minimization of these factors requires arriving at the lowest total of the above costs.

If purchasing departments had these costs quantified and available to buyers in a convenient form, lowest total cost decisions could be assured. This is not the case today, but this book will attempt to rectify the situation.

The importance of obtaining this information cannot be overemphasized, especially in cost trade-off situations. One such situation, which is very typical, occurs when a vendor with slower or less reliable delivery and, consequently, higher inventory and manufacturing costs for your company, will offer a lower price to entice a purchase. In this case, you must decide whether the lower price is a sufficient trade-off for the inefficiency of later delivery.

With information available on the impact of purchasing actions on all cost elements, you can be sure that, even in situations like the one above, your decisions will result in selection of the lowest material-cost alternative (illustrated by Option B in Figure 1). Without this information you can never be certain that you have attained the lowest cost possible.

Administrative-Cost Minimization

In addition to the need for material-cost minimization, information is required to relate material-cost effectiveness to administrative costs.

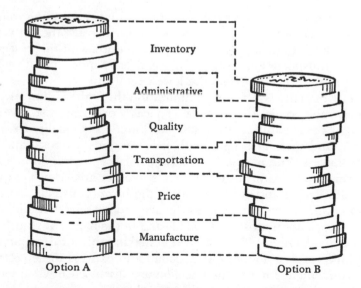

FIGURE 1. Maximum Value Equals Lowest Total Cost

This is the function of effective performance evaluation information and organization analysis. They must describe the minimization effectiveness of administrative dollars to identify the optimum administrative burden.

MATERIAL-COST DECISION CATEGORIES

In order to gain further direction in the most efficient approach to purchasing decisions and related information requirements, it is beneficial to subdivide material-related cost decisions into two categories: maintenance and improvement.

The maintenance decisions are those that even the least effective buyer must make daily in order to complete his clerical duties of order processing and his assurance-of-supply responsibilities. They are the decisions of vendor selection and expediting.

The improvement decisions require the buyer to stand back from the maintenance duties and identify the most effective methods of modifying normal buying practices to further minimize material-related costs. This is the creative, challenging aspect of the buyer's job that requires him to act rather than react to existing situations.

Maintenance Decisions

Making efficient maintenance decisions requires selecting vendors and expediting in a fashion that assures the least cost. Efficient vendor selection is more than simply choosing the vendor with the best price, terms, and transportation cost. As I have already indicated, it requires selecting the vendor that offers the lowest total cost.

In other words, to assure cost minimization through vendor selection, you must be able to identify the total applicable ordering cost, inventory cost, freight cost, manufacturing and stock-out costs, quality cost, cash terms cost, and price associated with each vendor's proposal and then select the lowest vendor cost alternative available to you. Some of this cost information is readily available, while in other areas, such as quality and manufacturing and stock-out costs, the buyer is usually left to his own intuition. However, to assure effective vendor selections, all of this total cost information must be available and in the hands of your buyers for their daily decisions. To assist you in making this information available, techniques describing how to obtain and express these costs in a manner convenient for vendor selection are discussed in Chapter 2 of this book.

Some of this cost information is also of value in structuring your expediting attack. Expediting is a mandatory part of a buying job since the buyer must get material delivered on time. However, expediting efficiency is critical; the buyer or expeditor has time limitations and cannot follow 100 percent of his outstanding orders effectively. To expedite efficiently, the buyer must have information available to enable him to develop his attack so that he concentrates the majority of his efforts on those vendors or materials most likely to present the greatest stock-out cost. Consequently, Chapter 2 also reviews a technique for obtaining and applying this cost information to provide assurance of supply.

Improvement Decisions

Performing maintenance duties effectively allows the buyer to keep his head above water, but it is the improvement portion of the buyer's job that is the justification for the professionalization of the buying function that has occurred over the last ten years. It is this area that seeks to go beyond the maintenance requirements to improve investment decisions by modifying existing buying procedures.

In most organizations, when a requirement for material is identified to purchasing, the following decisions have already been made by others: specifications of material, timing of required delivery, quantity to be ordered, whether material will be secured externally rather than internally, and whether material must be procured.

On receipt of quotations for the above specifications from your vendors, the price, transportation cost, and terms are also available. Maintenance decisions only involve selecting from existing vendor proposals and expediting the vendor, once selected, to assure that the delivery schedule is adequate. With sufficient total-cost information, these decisions are largely clerical.

Improvement decisions, however, require using vendor and market knowledge to question each of the decisions made by the other parts of the organization with respect to its total-cost contribution and value. Here is a typical list of the activities that purchasing applies in this questioning process:

1. *Redesign*
   a. Change in specification to meet industry standards rather than use of a special design
   b. Development of less restrictive specifications or procedures
   c. Utilization of alternate material (substitution) that performs the function required and results in lower total cost

      d. Standardization across commodity requirements
2. *Changing timing, ordering method, and quantity to be ordered*
    a. Extended contracting
        1. Term commitments
        2. System orders
        3. Vendor stocking
        4. Consignment buying
    b. Combining or splitting orders
    c. Quantity buy: Increase or decrease in order quantity to obtain quantity discount
    d. Price hedging: Buying excess material in anticipation of a price increase to achieve cost advantage
3. *Make-or-buy analysis*
    Change of fabrication point from internal to external or the reverse to achieve total-cost advantage
4. *Elimination of a purchase requirement*
    Use of material already inventoried; this action may involve (1) above
5. *New source development*

Each of these methods may be applicable in reducing one or all of the material-related costs that purchasing influences, but, without a judicious screening method, a wasteful amount of application time may also be involved.

SYSTEMATIC APPROACH TO IMPROVEMENT DECISIONS

Since the buyer has limited time for improvement activity, the crucial element in applying these techniques to achieve greater cost efficiency is not to just tell the buyer that the techniques are available and ask him to apply them (he would spend the rest of his time applying just one technique to all his commodities), but rather to direct him into the commodity-technique application that will yield the greatest benefit. In other words, you cannot just tell him to work harder and expect a maximum return. You must tell him how to work more intelligently.

> People . . . don't work any harder today than they did 50 years ago. There is à limited amount of improvement you can get from human effort. Once a person is giving full normal effort you can't expect more. The only way you can get continuous, cumulative productivity improvement is through changes in method. This is true whether you're

improving a product, a service, a job operation, a process or a system. The same guidelines apply.

The first guideline is to make the search for improvement systematic rather than merely opportunistic. With an opportunistic approach, improvement efforts will zero in on programs that obviously need doing and that offer the promise of lucrative results. Certainly we should make these obvious improvements, but the drawback of this kind of an approach is that it soon runs its course. Once you skim off the top layer of ready-made projects, the opportunities dwindle away.

But with a systematic approach, good improvements will continue to be discovered.[1]

Improvement Categories

In pursuing the objective of systematic application, the improvement activities should be divided into two groups on the basis of approach. In one of these groups, decision approaches are in sufficient detail that their application can be standardized across commodity lines. They can be applied on a gross basis justifying the minimal time expenditure required through a guaranteed return. Using priorities to approach these decisions is not necessary because the time expended will pay for itself.

For purposes of this discussion, the techniques in this category will be called "routine" improvement activities and will be grouped into the following classifications: combining or splitting orders, changing the order quantity, price hedging, elimination, and routine new source development.

The other group of improvement activities requires a substantial time expenditure for implementation and carries no guaranteed yield unless applied to only higher potential commodities. Consequently, these activities necessitate a selection technique to avoid unproductive allocation of administrative cost. In this discussion, improvement techniques that require this approach will be called "keying" activities and will include redesign, make-or-buy, contracting, and active new source development.

Routine Activities

The detailed application of routine improvement activities is discussed in Chapter 3. However, a brief review of the nature of these activities is provided below.

The *combining* or *splitting* of orders, except when initiated in a contracting activity, can be handled routinely as you perform your maintenance

---

[1]Excerpts from a speech made by D. C. Burnham, chairman of the Westinghouse Electric Corporation, at Carnegie-Mellon University, November 15, 1972.

duties with a minimal additional time expenditure. Combining requisitions into one order should be done at any time possible when required dates on requisitions are similar and one vendor is capable of efficiently providing the combined material requirement. Splitting should be pursued only when there is a cost advantage large enough to offset the additional purchase order processing cost. The valuation process to assist in identifying whether the savings justifies the expense is the key to effective combining or splitting and is discussed in Chapter 3.

If required dates are dissimilar and combination still appears productive, the situation parallels that of investigating *quantity-break advantages*. Tables are provided in Chapter 3 to minimize the complexity and time expended in this activity. The quantity-break decision for each group of commodities, once determined, need be revised only when quantity breaks change. Again, a significant yield can be obtained with minimal time expense through pursuit of this activity.

Price hedging is called for only when the price will change and presents a guaranteed-yield opportunity that should not be ignored. Methods of obtaining the necessary data and determining the quantity to be hedged (brought in or ordered early) in the face of a price increase are also discussed in Chapter 3. As with the quantity break these methods include tables to reduce the complexity usually associated with this decision.

Nonroutine Activities

In order to efficiently apply the nonroutine techniques additional direction is required. Unlike the routine improvement activities, these techniques carry no guaranteed yield unless implemented with discretion. In order to assure that the time expended in these efforts carries the greatest potential benefit, it is necessary to steer application towards the commodities with the highest potential.

This direction can be gained through use of the material-related costs that were discussed in conjunction with the maintenance duties. By rank-ordering your commodities based on highest total material-related cost per annum, you can identify those having the greatest potential. Improvement activities applied to the highest total-cost commodities will supply the greatest cost benefit. Consequently, the techniques that follow require that improvement applications be pursued initially on the highest rank commodities applicable to your technique. However, identifying which of the remaining improvement techniques will produce the greatest return for a specific highest cost commodity requires further discussion.

Keying and Routine

New source development, depending on the specific application, may be approached routinely as a daily duty or on a special project basis. A routine application would be in conjunction with interviewing untried vendors to solicit a quotation on your highest total-cost commodity in the vendor's product line. This is an informal approach to developing new sources and making vendor interviews more productive, but does require being able to identify this highest cost commodity to assure the most beneficial application for both you and the vendor. Chapter 3 describes this approach and the creation and use of tools to aid in its effective implementation.

The keying or special project improvement approach to new source development is applied by actively pursuing new sources to effect minimization. This should be the top-priority improvement activity for those highest-cost commodities that are source-controlled or sole-source; in most cases, the potential payoff in these commodities will be maximized by engaging in new source development rather than alternate improvement techniques. This situation exists because of a lack of competitive policing ability and lack of incentive for the vendor to recommend lower-cost alternatives in these types of commodities.

Keying Activities

The method used to key (direct) your efforts towards active pursuit of new sources for your highest-cost commodities was the lack of existing alternate sources. If alternate sources exist, however, a more formalized keying approach is required to allow you to select the optimum improvement activity of those remaining: redesign, contracting, and make-or-buy. The recommended method here is to concentrate — or "key" — on the activity that offers the greatest yield with respect to your highest-cost commodity.

To gain this direction, you could estimate the potential yield available through each technique. Estimating methods are discussed in subsequent chapters. However, due to the time that would be required to identify target yields for each one of these techniques with respect to each of your major-cost commodities, an alternate approach is recommended.

In analyzing each activity, you can identify the highest potential improvement technique based on the cost structure of your highest-cost commodities and the relative values of the cost influences of each technique. It must be recognized that any one of the activities — redesign, make-or-buy, or contracting — could potentially reduce any or all of the relative-cost areas. However, certain of these activities will hold more promise for affecting given cost areas than others.

For instance, *redesign*, including change to industry standard, change to less restrictive procedures, substitution of materials, and commodity standardization, could potentially affect inventory, stock-out, transportation, and utilization costs, but its primary application when compared to the other techniques will be in reducing the cost contributions related to price and quality.

Contracting has the greatest potential compared to the other alternatives in reducing the costs of inventory, ordering, and vendor profit, in that the extended commitment usually involved in contracting offers a vendor efficiencies in these cost areas. Doubtless, contracting can affect price as well, but its impact is similar to that of quantity procurement (price-breaks) which should be pursued on a routine basis as proposed above and not conducted sporadically.

Make-or-buy, on the other hand, has the greatest potential for reducing the total of your manufacturing cost and price of material. In pursuing make-or-buy, purchasing has the unique opportunity of letting outside vendors' technical people look at methods of satisfying your functional requirements with both alternate materials and manufacturing methods to promote improvement in these costs.

In applying this analysis, it is possible to identify which of the above approaches to improvement has the greatest potential for any given commodity by adding the commodity's relative costs most likely to be affected by each technique. This process is illustrated below:

Redesign:	1.	Price
	2.	Quality
Make-or-buy:	1.	Price
	2.	Manufacturing
	3.	Profit restricted by capacity
Contracting:	1.	Ordering
	2.	Vendor profit
	3.	Inventory

With this information, the optimum improvement technique for application on any commodity is easily identified. It will be the technique that can influence the greatest proportion of cost associated with that commodity.

After identification and application of the most beneficial improvement technique, target yield information is also required to assure that, through negotiation, you will achieve full value. The specific methods for developing these targets and gathering the above information is explained in Chapter 4.

PERFORMANCE EVALUATION: APPROACH TO IMPROVEMENT

A key feature of this information system and improvement approach has been omitted to this point. This is performance evaluation. None of the techniques described so far will indicate whether or not your improvement activities have been effective, or whether additional or fewer staff personnel are necessary to achieve administrative and improvement efficiency. The aforementioned techniques by themselves also provide little ability to plan for improvement or motivate people towards improvement objectives. These failings can all be solved through an effective performance-evaluation program.

With performance evaluation included, the total approach to improvement could be depicted as follows:

1. Evaluate present minimization performance.
2. Review potential improvement available in reducing costs on major cost commodities.
3. Set objectives.
4. Select and apply improvement activities.
5. Evaluate minimization performance to reestablish objectives and activities.

Items 2 and 4 above can be provided through activities already discussed, but the soundness of the approach depends on identifying performance efficiency, charting an improvement course, and evaluating its effectiveness.

Establish Objectives

There are basically two approaches that may be used to set objectives. One does not require the application of step 2 (above), but both require prior performance evaluation to set the standard for improvement.

The approach not requiring a review of potential improvement (step 2) is more widely applied in industry but offers a less complete goal-setting directive. In this approach, based on performance history and an intuitive feel for what improvements are available, an objective is established. The problem with this technique is that when it comes time to reevaluate that objective, it is extremely difficult to judge whether the objective was faulty or performance was just better or worse than expected.

A more comprehensive approach, which not only identifies a desired improvement level but also relates this goal to specific projects and the potential improvement of each, would be to request each buyer to review his highest cost commodities, to identify priority-improvement projects for each of these commodities, and to total the cost yields expected from each application. By using this information to build the improvement objective, it is possible to specify the goal to each buyer and section, promoting goal commitment in buyers and enabling you to evaluate performance against objective.

Evaluating Performance Against Objectives

Evaluating performance against objectives is critical not only in reviewing vendors' and individuals' performance in order to identify improvement progress, but also in planning for greater staffing efficiency. It is this step that can display the performance consequences of organizations with respect to clerical load, and that will answer the question: "What improvement level would have been possible with additional or fewer people, to increase or decrease the time available for improvement rather than clerical duties?" This will serve to identify the desirable balance between salary levels and improvement yield.

Organization of Responsibility

Finally, in this decision system, we must also decide how to identify the organization that will promote the greatest efficiency in all these activities. Without the proper organization of responsibilities, you will find it impossible to achieve the lowest total cost; for you will be forced to employ more people than necessary to obtain the same results available from an alternate form of organization. To select the organization that is right for you, you must address these questions:

1. *Product Line Versus Commodity Buying*. Will better results be obtained by assigning a buyer responsibility for procuring all of the commodities within one of my company's product lines, or by assigning one buyer responsibility for a commodity included in many product lines?
2. *Centralized Versus Decentralized Buying*. Will better results be ob-

tained by centralizing this buying so that expertise is concentrated, or by decentralizing to provide greater service to each of the producing locations?

Each of these questions involves many considerations and, for this reason, it is difficult both to reach and to justify the correct decision.

To assist you in structuring this effort, Chapter 6 provides techniques for arriving at the best decision and supporting your conclusion to management.

SUMMARY

This total decision technique can be visualized as a circle (Figure 2), beginning and ending with performance evaluation, applied initially in goal setting and finally in evaluating performance against goals. Proceeding around this circle, the smallest completed loop includes performance evaluation and the *maintenance* activities of vendor selection and expediting. These activities are the minimum in which a respectable purchasing operation must engage.

The information required to make effective maintenance decisions was that depicting total material-related cost. In applying this informa-

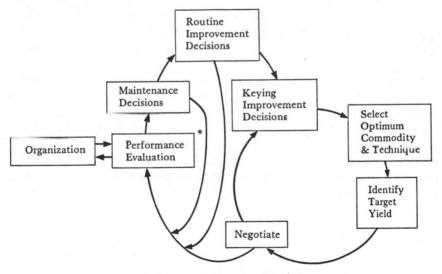

*Begin with Performance Evaluation

FIGURE 2. Decision System Summary

tion, vendor selection should be made on the basis of the lowest total-cost proposal, and expediting activities should be put in priority with respect to those vendors contributing the potential stock-out cost (an element of material-related cost). Information will be provided in Chapter 2 that describes methods to efficiently provide the necessary cost data and apply it to this daily decision-making process.

The next largest loop includes the *routine improvement* activities of price hedging, quantity buying, elimination of ordering requirements, combining or splitting orders, and pursuing new source development through vendor interviewing. Engaging in these activities will produce a guaranteed yield and justify the time commitment required. Decision approaches can be formalized and standardized so that the necessary time commitment is minimal. Application of these activities is discussed in Chapter 3.

The largest loop includes the more sophisticated improvement activities that require *keying* techniques. The keying technique involves initiating activity on the highest total-cost commodity, and steering the activity into either contracting, respecification, or make or buy, based on the material-related cost composition of that commodity.

After the optimum activity is identified, a target yield should be decided on for use in the final step of negotiation. Methods for assigning these target yields and for the keying process are discussed in Chapter 4.

Going through this process with the data identified will set the stage for obtaining the lowest material-related cost, the primary goal of purchasing. However, to assure that you will achieve this objective, the cycle must be completed with performance evaluation. Chapter 5 describes how to use this tool in motivating buyers to pursue these activities aggressively.

Finally, to obtain lowest total cost you must also be able to make effective organizational decisions. These decisions assure that procurement responsibility is divided so that the fewest number of people are required to obtain the greatest possible results, and when combined with performance evaluation enable you to identify the exact number of people needed to achieve these results. Chapter 6 reviews the means to minimize administrative cost through identifying the best organization for your operation.

2

Maintenance Decisions: Vendor Selection and Expediting Prioritization

We initiate the discussion of this decision-making process with a review of the maintenance decisions. The information used in these decisions, the most frequent ones in purchasing, will be necessary not only to efficient vendor selection and expediting but in other decision areas as well. Let us begin with a review of the maintenance-decision objectives and the problems that currently exist in meeting these objectives.

As was discussed in Chapter 1, the primary requirement in effectively performing maintenance duties is selecting and expediting vendors on the basis of their total material-related cost contribution. Certain of these material-related costs appear easy to evaluate, since they are highly visible within the context of the vendor's quotation. These visible costs and cost influences are net price (price minus cash discounts), freight, and promise date (vendor leadtime). However, the other cost influences, those related to quality and delivery, are hidden in the vendor's past and expected future performance.

This hidden cost situation puts the inexperienced buyer at a decided disadvantage. Since he has no experience with his vendors' performances, he is only capable of using the visible factors in his decisionmaking. As a result, when selecting vendors, this buyer will arrive at decisions in the following manner. If the promise dates are nearly the same or both offers fall within the required leadtime, the vendor with the lowest net price and freight will receive the award. If, however, one vendor's promise jeopardizes the required leadtime but also represents the lowest visible cost proposal, two courses of action are possible. The buyer may attempt to negotiate the leadtime promise (even though he is not certain that even the original promise can be met), or he may place the order with the vendor offering the shortest promise but higher cost. In none of these instances will he deal effectively with the costs related to quality or unreliable delivery.

In expediting activities, the inexperienced buyer is in an even worse position, for he has no way of identifying which of his vendors' promise dates are likely to be upheld. Thus, instead of expediting unreliable vendors in advance of their promise dates in order to assure timely supply, this buyer is forced to assume that all vendors will deliver as promised, and to expedite only after the vendor has not met his expectation. Consequently, rather than acting to minimize the possibility of late delivery, the inexperienced buyer can only react after this possibility has become a reality. As you can see, if information and techniques are not available to compensate for this buyer's lack of experience, his decisions will not meet the objective of lowest material-related cost, because he will be unable to gauge the significance of hidden costs.

The experienced buyer still has a need for the same information and techniques, not to guide his decisions but to support and refine them. In order to clarify this need, let us review the process and results of learning through experience.

The experienced buyer has learned which of his vendors are most likely to present insufficient quality or unreliable delivery problems. He learns to combine this information in his decisionmaking with a trial-and-error solution method which will be titled the "squeaky wheel" technique.

The squeaky wheel technique is illustrated in the following example. The buyer in making previous decisions might have selected a lowest net price and freight vendor due to a cost-reduction push or lack of experience, even though this vendor had a history of late delivery or insufficient quality. As well, he may have ignored advance expediting completely once the order was placed. If the resulting "flak level" was low, the buyer would intuitively identify this commodity as having a net-price and freight-cost priority, and would see no reason to modify his approach to vendor selection and expediting. If, however, he was rebuked for late delivery or inadequate quality, priority would be placed with either delivery or quality rather than with the other costs. After a number of these experiences, the intelligent buyer automatically stays out of trouble by sorting commodities into quality, delivery or other cost priority, by grouping vendors in accordance with their capability, and by selecting and expediting vendors with respect to the highest priority-capability match. This process is slow and depends on learning from mistakes, but given time and intelligent buyers, it will provide excellent results. However, even when the buyer has learned to make effective decisions he still requires information to support his conclusions, which are based on intuitive costs difficult for one not having the same experiences to understand and support. Without supporting information this buyer may be prevented from making decisions that he knows are correct.

Further, even in making the basic decisions with respect to the visible costs of net price and freight in vendor selection, certain additional cost adjustments are necessary to assure optimum decisions. Few buyers, even experienced ones, take these adjustments into consideration. For instance, when considering terms of payment, a 2 percent/10 net 30 discount compared to a net 30 term does not result in a 2 percent savings. Since paying in 10 days rather than 30 costs your company money, the effective savings or price offset will be less significant than 2 percent. Ignoring this cost offset can lead to poor decisions.

Freight costs can also be misleading and require adjustment before making effective decisions. Anticipated freight costs are usually based on an estimate obtained from considering the lowest rate available between destinations. If, however, you recurringly require premium shipment as a result of vendor lateness or insufficient leadtime, this lowest-rate comparison will be meaningless.

As an illustration of the bias resulting from using the lowest possible rates in your decisions, consider the data in Figure 3. These data have been obtained for the same commodity from actual raw-material freight bills that were paid over a period of two months. The lowest or prime rates from each vendor are circled and destinations are designated by numbers while vendors are depicted alphabetically.

As you can see, the prime rate for vendor B is lower than that for vendor A ($3.60 compared to $4.00). If these rates provide the basis for

FIGURE 3. Freight Cost Examples

Vendor	Destina-tion	Tons	Month 1 Rate/ton	Avg./ton	Tons	Month 2 Rate/ton	Avg./ton
A	1	12	6.00	6.00	7	(4.00)	4.59
					20	4.80	
B	1	24	4.00	4.53	10	5.00	4.63
		48	4.40		3	4.80	
		2	13.20		1	4.60	
		29	4.60		4	4.40	
					3	(3.60)	

your decision, vendor B would receive a clear advantage. Yet, as is evident above in the second month, the actual average rate was higher for B than for A and in neither month did the actual average rate come within 15 percent of the prime. This is only one example but was typical of 80 different rate vendor combinations that were reviewed.

In order to overcome these blocks to effective decisionmaking, a framework is required that will allow the experienced, effective buyer to support his intuitive judgment and will guide the inexperienced or ineffective buyer's decisions to yield lowest-cost results. This chapter will provide this framework by the following method:

1. Providing a means of adjusting terms of payment and freight to reflect actual savings and costs.
2. Defining, gathering, and portraying the hidden costs for each vendor as experienced by past performance in quality, delivery, and cost improvement contribution.
3. Describing how to use this information to minimize material-related cost in selecting your vendors and expediting your priorities.

In conjunction with enabling you to make decisions about lowest material-related costs, this system will also allow you to provide and use this information at a minimal expense in buyer and clerical time.

The discussion of this system begins with a procedure to adjust terms of payment to reflect net savings. It continues by describing a data-collection method that will allow you to obtain accurate freight, quality, delivery, and improvement contribution cost factors for each significant vendor. And it ends with a procedure which enables you to apply this information efficiently in expediting and vendor selection.

TERMS-OF-PAYMENT VALUATION

In negotiating or valuing vendor offers, it is important to realize that cash discounts such as 2/10 net 30 when compared to net terms will not provide a savings equal to the offered percent discount. In fact, some of these discounts are of no value at all, since taking advantage of them through early payment costs you more than the discount saves. This situation exists because an offsetting cost is required to take advantage of discount terms. Vendors offer discounts, in part, to insure prompt payment and reduce their borrowing requirements. Taking advantage of the discount by paying early creates borrowing costs for your company.

In the same manner, progress payments will also increase your borrowing costs and decrease the value of a vendor's offer. In order to assure that you make the best vendor selection, these borrowing costs must be considered in valuing the terms-of-payment offerings that you receive.

Discount and Payment Delays

The formulas that will enable you to determine the savings available from discounts and payment delays (net terms) are displayed below:

Equation 1

$$\text{Discount Savings} = \frac{D\% + \left(\frac{IA\%}{360} \cdot D_d\right)}{100}$$

where: $D\%$ = percentage of discount available for early payment

IA = percentage of company borrowing cost

D_d = days in which payment must be made to receive $D\%$

Equation 2

$$\text{Net Terms Savings} = \frac{\frac{IA\%}{360} \cdot N_d}{100}$$

where: N_d = days in which net payment is due

These formulas are not complicated, but the consecutive calculations required when a buyer uses them to value proposals adds an unnecessary burden. It is very easy to precalculate the results of these formulas as in Table 1.

By making this table available to your buyers, they can value any term shown simply by:

1. Finding the quoted terms of payment in Column 1.
2. Referring across this row to Column 2 to identify the decimal savings offered by this term.[1]
3. Continuing to Column 3 to identify if the discount should be taken or if payment should be made in accordance with the net-day option.

[1]To convert to dollars, multiply this decimal times price.

TABLE 1. Discount and Payment Delay Savings[1]

Typical Terms	Decimal Savings[2]	Is Discount Worthwhile?
Cash	0.0	—
Net 30	0.008	—
1/4% 10 Net 30	0.008	No
1/2% 10 Net 30	0.008	No
3/4% 10 Net 30	0.010	Yes
3/4% 10 Net 60	0.017	No
3/4% 30 Net 60	0.017	No
1% 10 Net 30	0.013	Yes
1% 10 Net 60	0.017	No
1% 30 Net 60	0.018	Yes
1% 30 Net 90	0.025	No
Net 60	0.017	—
2% 10 Net 30	0.023	Yes
2% 10 Net 60	0.023	Yes
2% 10 Net 90	0.025	No
2% 30 Net 60	0.028	Yes
2% 30 Net 90	0.028	Yes
Net 90	0.025	—

[1] Savings are computed using a 10 percent company borrowing rate. To modify this table for inclusion of additional terms or use of a borrowing cost other than 10 percent refer to Appendix 1 for instructions.

[2] For prox. or EOM terms: add 0.004 to the savings for the applicable term referenced.

Consequently, with this table you can be sure that your buyers are able to efficiently cost vendor-discount and payment-delay offers.

Progress Payments

Use of a similar approach will also enable you to simplify the identification of costs associated with proposed progress payments. In this approach, as well, a precalculated table is offered. However, a different type of table is required because there are two significant differences between payment delays and progress payments. First, progress payments produce a cost to your company rather than a savings. Second, payment delay terms pertain to the total cost of the material ordered whereas progress payments are usually applicable to only a percentage of this total. In order to account for these differences, the previous "Net Terms Savings" equation must be modified as shown below to determine the cost of progress payments:

Equation 3

$$\text{Progress Payment Cost} = \sum_{x=1}^{n} \frac{IA}{360} \cdot P_x \cdot D_x$$

where: IA = company borrowing cost (decimal)
P_x = percentage of total payment due for progress payment (x) (decimal)
x = payment number 1, 2 .... n
n = total number of progress payments
D_x = number of days prior to shipment that payment (x) is due.

As with payment delays, however, you will find it much less time-consuming to apply Table 2, which precalculates $\left(\frac{IA}{360} \cdot D_x \cdot P_x \right)$ for various D_x and P_x values.

In using this table, to value progress payments, a buyer need only:

1. Identify the number of days prior to shipment of material (D_x) on which each progress payment is due, and the percentage of total material cost due for each payment.

For example:

		Days due prior to shipment (D_x)	% Due (P_x)
Vendor A	Payment 1 Payment 2	100 days 50 days	30% 20%

2. Value the cost of each payment by locating the applicable cost factor in Table 2.

For example:

		Cost Factor from Table 2
Payment 1 Payment 2	Since (D_x) = 100 and (P_x) = 30% Since (D_x) = 50 and (P_x) = 20%	.0084 .0028

3. Total these cost factors to identify the total (decimal) progress payment per vendor[1].

[1] This factor may be converted to dollars by multiplying times price.

TABLE 2. Progress Payment Cost Factor[1] Table[2]

Number of Days Prior to Shipment on Which Each Payment Is Due (D_x)	Percentage of Payment Due For Each Payment (P_x)										
	5%	10%	20%	30%	40%	50%	60%	70%	80%	90%	100%
10	.00015	.0003	.0006	.0009	.0012	.0015	.0018	.0021	.0024	.0027	.0030
20	.0003	.0006	.0012	.0018	.0024	.0030	.0036	.0042	.0048	.0054	.0060
30	.0004	.0008	.0016	.0024	.0032	.0040	.0048	.0056	.0064	.0072	.008
40	.0006	.0011	.0022	.0033	.0044	.0055	.0066	.0077	.0088	.0099	.011
50	.0007	.0014	.0028	.0042	.0056	.0070	.0084	.0098	.0112	.0126	.014
60	.0008	.0017	.0034	.0051	.0068	.0085	.0102	.0119	.0136	.0153	.017
70	.0010	.0019	.0038	.0057	.0076	.0095	.0114	.0133	.0152	.0171	.019
80	.0011	.0022	.0044	.0066	.0088	.011	.0132	.0154	.0176	.0198	.022
90	.0012	.0025	.0050	.0075	.0100	.0125	.0150	.0175	.0200	.0225	.025
100	.0014	.0028	.0056	.0084	.0112	.014	.0168	.0196	.0224	.0252	.028
200	.0028	.0056	.0112	.0168	.0224	.028	.0336	.0392	.0448	.0504	.056
300	.0042	.0083	.0166	.0249	.0332	.0415	.0498	.0581	.0664	.0747	.083

[1] Caclulated using 10 percent borrowing cost.
[2] To modify this table for costs other than 10 percent, multiply each cost factor by the following ratio:
(Your Borrowing Cost ÷ 10 percent)

For example:

Payment 1 = .0084 Cost Factor
Payment 2 = .0028 Cost Factor
Therefore, total progress payment cost = .0112 or 1.12 percent.

As you can see, by applying these two procedures and tables your buyers can quickly identify the actual value of any terms-of-payment offer. Consequently, with these techniques, you can assure that terms-of-payment decisions are consistent with your lowest-total-cost objective.

COST DEFINITION AND DATA COLLECTION FOR FREIGHT AND HIDDEN-COST FACTORS

Since terms of payment are included in vendor quotations, the buyer need do no more than refer to these quotations and value the terms as instructed by the previous procedure. However, the cost incurred as a result of the other factors will depend on the vendor's performance with respect to his quoted commitments, and it cannot be determined without supplementary performance data. Consequently, as we have discussed, it is necessary to approximate these costs in order to provide a framework for effective vendor selection and expediting.

The approximation method suggested in this chapter uses historical costs in a manner similar to that applied by the experienced buyer, and projects those costs into the future for decision-making purposes. In order to provide this approximation, it is necessary first to define how these factors have affected costs, and then to depict these effects in a convenient form.

Cost Definition

Before reviewing data-collection and valuation procedures, we must first identify the information significant to each of these hidden-cost contributors. Let us begin with a discussion of freight costs.

Freight

In some instances, freight costs will be visible in the quotation and will require no additional analysis. If your freight terms are "allowed," the freight charges will be firm within your vendor's quoted price and the cost will be clearly defined. Likewise, if freight is included as a separate but firm portion of a vendor's quotation, the exact cost of transportation will be readily available.

If, however, your terms are "not allowed" and a firm price for freight is not quoted, you must take further steps to estimate the effective freight rate and reach a sound, lowest-cost decision. Obtaining an accurate estimate of this cost requires being able to predict for each vendor whether the material, in order to meet your delivery requirements, will be shipped by premium or lowest-cost transportation.

This prediction can best be provided by discovering the vendor's historical average freight cost between destinations. A separate individual analysis for each purchase would require an exorbitant administrative expense. However, this summary measure provides an excellent substitute. It not only quickly and easily displays a vendor's actual past freight performance and your related historical cost, but this history also provides a sound basis for estimating future effective costs in vendor selection. Consequently, the information of significance to freight-cost evaluation is found in the vendor's freight-payment history.

Cost-Improvement Contribution

Another vendor-cost characteristic that must be valued, along with price, terms of payment, and freight, is the contribution that the vendor makes in reducing your costs. This factor is also absent from the vendor's quotation, but can be very significant to your performance. Vendors are experts in their commodity lines and in the factors that affect their costs. They can be valuable sources of useful ideas that affect the price, delivery, and quality of your purchase. The vendors that are working to match their system with yours to offer you the greatest value for your material dollar should be given credit for this èffort in your vendor-selection program for two reasons. First, you will be able to evaluate the actual cost of doing business with that vendor. Second, it will spur even further initiative on his part and the part of non-contributory vendors by rewarding their efforts.

In order to be in a position to provide this credit, it is necessary to accumulate data on past cost-improvement contributions by vendors and to apply these data in your vendor-selection practice.

Delivery-Related Cost Valuation

It is also necessary to review the value effected by a vendor's delivery performance. There are two basic types of commodity, delivery-related characteristics that influence your costs: leadtime (vendor promise), and lack of leadtime reliability. Both of these characteristics are controllable by your vendors and influenced by purchasing through the activities of vendor selection, expediting and the method of ordering.

The commodity leadtime directly affects the amount of material that must be held in inventory to maintain operations until a replenishment order can be received, but lack of leadtime reliability affects both assurance of supply and inventory cost. For purposes of this discussion, lack of reliability is subdivided into two categories based on cost impact: early shipment and late shipment.

An early shipment assures that material is received in time, but results in a higher inventory than desired because the material that has been shipped and received early must be stored for a longer period than planned. Consequently, the cost associated with early shipment will be a function of the number of days shipped early and the value of the shipment.

Late shipments will jeopardize production schedules and, as with the other factors, have an influence on inventory costs. Since necessary replenishment-stock levels and ordering leadtimes are calculated using the "promised" leadtimes, an unplanned increase in this leadtime through late delivery will increase "stock-outs" to an undesirable level. To prevent these undesired stock-outs, it is necessary to stock additional material with a consequent increase in inventory costs. In holding the vendor responsible for late delivery, he must be held accountable for meeting his promise date, since this is one of the key elements applied in vendor selection and thus is critical to minimizing material-related costs.

The cost associated with these delivery delays will be dependent on the number of days late and the frequency of late delivery. If the material is only a few days late, minor rescheduling or available schedule slack will usually be enough to compensate. However, if the period is extreme, much higher adjustment costs will be incurred. Similarly, as the number of shipment delays increases in its relation to total shipments (frequency of delay), the costs incurred will also increase.

In summary, information of significance to a vendor's delivery-related cost contribution can be displayed as follows:

1. Leadtime
2. Lack of leadtime reliability
    a. Early shipment
        1) Days early
        2) Value of shipment
    b. Late shipment
        1) Days late
        2) Percentage of shipments late

Leadtime is readily available in the quotation in the form of the vendor's promise. However, in order to make cost-minimizing decisions with regard to the other factors, the above data must be collected on a historical basis to facilitate a cost approximation.

Quality Cost-Identification Claims Valuation

Quality-related costs are also important considerations in materials evaluation, both in vendor selection and application of improvement techniques. The two major groupings of quality costs can be classified as follows:

1. Cost of assuring sufficient quality
    a. Vendor risk charges
    b. Vendor testing charges
2. Cost related to insufficient quality
    a. Direct costs incurred in identification and repair
        1) Labor
        2) Processing
    b. Delivery delays resulting from not having usable material

The first category, "cost of assuring sufficient quality," represents very real costs. However, these costs are included in the price of material or as "extra" charges quoted directly with the material. Although these costs are not always identifiable, separate from price, their inclusion with price makes them an integral part of evaluation of vendor offerings without the need for supplemental information. The ability to separate these costs from price is helpful in determining the application direction of improvement techniques and methods to accomplish this separation will be covered in Chapter 4.

However, application of these separation techniques is recommended only in select instances to avoid wasted time and, therefore, elaboration is not suitable for this maintenance-duty discussion.

Costs related to the second category, "cost related to insufficient quality," are not available within the vendor's quotation. Consequently, further effort is necessary to include this cost in your valuation.

The two types of cost influences resulting from insufficient quality are direct costs and late deliveries. If a vendor's insufficient quality is identified prior to use of the material, the material will be returned or shipment stopped and a replacement requested. Thus, a delivery delay results.

If work has already begun or been completed on the material when the defect is identified, the applicable costs will be reflected by claims issued to collect the labor charges incurred, the cost of the defective material, and the costs of complete inspection and processing. Here, there will also be a delivery delay caused by the reworking or replacing of material.

Costs of delivery delays were already discussed. However, elaboration is required with respect to claim costs. If the claim value is accurate, the costs you have incurred from vendor error, your claim, can and will eventually be recovered. Assuming a valid claim exists, the effective direct cost incurred by the company as a result of vendor error is not the dollar value of the claim but instead the financing charges necessary to support that claim value until it is collected. In effect, the claim is a form of buyer-vendor trade credit.

In order to value the financing charges caused by claims, it is necessary to identify the dollar value of claims by vendor and the period outstanding for each claim. It is these factors that will determine the necessary interest charges, for use in vendor selection.

Data Collection

To this point in our review, we have delineated the cost influences of terms of payment, freight, cost improvement contribution, delivery, and quality. We have concluded that with the exception of terms of payment, more information than that available in the vendor's quotation is required to identify the cost contribution related to these factors. The historical information requirements that were identified can be summarized as follows:

    I.   Claims
         A.   Dollar value of outstanding claims
         B.   Average time outstanding
   II.   Early shipment
         A.   Dollar value of early shipment
         B.   Average time received early (required date minus receipt date)
  III.   Cost improvement
         A.   Vendor's dollar value of contribution
   IV.   Freight
         A.   Dollar total of freight bills
    V.   Leadtime
         A.   Quoted promise date
   VI.   Late delivery costs
         A.   Percentage of orders late
             1.   Number of orders late

        a.   As a result of quality defect
        b.   As a result of other causes
   2.   Number of orders due
B.   Average time late

If you are fortunate enough to have much of this historical information in your computer files, identifiable to the contributing vendor, perhaps in order-status records, data collection does not present a major problem. This information can be provided automatically by computerizing the following collection and valuation process for all your vendors.

However, if information must be compiled manually, a simplifying technique must be applied to prevent excessive clerical expense. The technique proposed involves classification of "significant" vendors in order to limit the computation required, and formalization of a data-collection procedure for efficient clerical application. By following the procedures outlined below, this information has been collected for a department handling 15,000 orders per year at an expense of only four hours per month clerical time.

Significant-Vendor Identification

Collection of all these measures for every vendor that you might do business with could be a lifetime project. However, if we classify vendors with respect to significance to our performance, we find that only a few are critical to our objectives. The trick in this identification is the establishing of critical-noncritical decision rules. Two are proposed below.

The first rule pertains to collection of all but the late delivery information. This technique works with an assumption, empirically verified in numerous situations, that 10 percent of your vendors will account for approximately 80 percent of your dollars purchased. With this assumption, it should be clear that the vendors whose cost is of most significance to your department performance will be those few vendors who are responsible for the greatest proportion of your dollars. Consequently you are best advised, in order to limit collection expense, to concentrate on these key vendors in your collection effort. In applying this advice, you should collect the claims, early shipment, cost improvement, and freight information referenced above only for those vendors who are significant from a dollar standpoint.

Further, your computation of the delivery information will not be very meaningful unless you have a representative number of orders per vendor on which to develop the statistics. As an illustration, if three orders are placed with a vendor and one is delivered late, this does not necessarily indicate that the same vendor will consistently deliver 2/3 of the orders on time. The one overdue might not occur for another 10 orders. With such a small number of observations, the buyer's intuitive judgment about shipment reliability would be much more useful than any statistic and could be obtained easily from a review of the orders themselves. However, as the number of orders rises, the statistic will be much more representative of expected future performance and easier to apply than an order review by the buyer. Consequently, an additional narrowing technique related to the collection of delivery information is recommended. If you do not place more than eight orders per year with a vendor, it is suggested that you collect none of this delivery information for that vendor; his effect on your delivery performance will be relatively insignificant.

Following these two "narrowing" rules, as supported by actual data-collection efforts, has resulted in reducing the number of orders reviewed by 30 percent for the total existent in the department and the number of vendors for whom data are collected to 10 percent of those active in order receipts.

Once you have identified significant vendors, you should then create a sheet like Form 1 for each of these vendors and maintain this sheet as a permanent record for ease of collection and summary of data.

Manual Data Collection

Efficient manual data collection and analysis requires more than the above significant vendor rules. It also requires a preprinted form and detailed instructions concerning by whom and from what documents information should be collected, how it should be displayed on the form, and how to analyze displayed information. To this end Form 1 is offered and discussed in three segments based on the point of information collection. These segments include:

1. Information collected from the purchase order (columns 1 through 10)
2. Information collected from claims (columns 12 through 16)
3. Information from vendor cost-improvement contributions (column 19)

Even if you are planning to collect information via computer, it will be worth your while to review these manual collection systems for the general orientation provided.

Let us begin this collection review with the most time-consuming portion, information collected from the purchase order.

FORM 1. Vendor Performance Data-Collection Form

1	2	3	4	5	6	7	8	9	10	11	12	13	14
PURCHASE ORDER NUMBER	VENDOR'S FIRST PROMISE DATE	FINAL RECEIPT DATE	WEEKS OVERDUE	WEEKS EARLY	TOTAL NUMBER OF SHIPMENT	NUMBER OF SHIPMENT REJECTED	TOTAL EARLY SHIP VALUE	TOTAL SHIPMENT VALUE	TOTAL FREIGHT	DELIVERY ANALYSIS	WORK SPACE	CLAIMS VALUE	CLAIMS VENDOR NOTIFICATION DATE
										EARLY SHIP COST			
										FIND AVERAGE TIME EARLY			
										DIVIDE:			
										TOTAL COLUMN 5 / NUMBER ENTRIES COLUMN 5			
										APPLY TABLE USING AVERAGE TIME EARLY AND TOTAL IN COLUMN 8			

PURCHASE-ORDER DATA COLLECTION.   Recording the information required from the closed purchase order will require less than fifteen seconds per order in addition to your normal order-closeout review. In accordance with this procedure and on review of the closed order, it is necessary to record:

1. Purchase order number (column 1)
2. Vendor's first promise date (column 2)
3. Final receipt date (column 3), defined as the date on which acceptable material was received complete
4. Total number of shipments (column 6)
5. Number of shipments rejected (column 7)
6. Total shipment value (column 9)
7. Total freight value (column 10)

For the great majority of orders, there will be only one shipment and

VENDOR NAME: Vendor X Z

15	16	17	18	19	20	21
CLAIMS CLOSE-OUT DATE	WEEKS OUT-STANDING	CLAIMS ANALYSIS	WORK SPACE	COST IMPROVEMENT CONTRIBUTION	CONSOLIDATED ANALYSIS	WORK SPACE
		AVERAGE WEEKS OUTSTANDING			TOTAL:	
		DIVIDE:			(COLUMN 10) - (EARLY SHIP COST) - (CLAIMS COST) - (COLUMN 19)	
		TOTAL COLUMN 16 / NO. ENTRIES COLUMN 16				
					COST RATIO	
		CLAIMS COST			DIVIDE:	
		APPLY TABLE USING AVERAGE WEEKS OUTSTANDING AND CLAIM TOTAL COLUMN (19)			ABOVE TOTAL / COLUMN 9 TOTAL	
					LATE DELIVERY	
					% OVERDUE RATIO	
					DIVIDE:	
					NUMBER ENTRIES COLUMN (4) / NUMBER ENTRIES COLUMN (1)	
					AVERAGE TIME OVERDUE	
					DIVIDE:	
					TOTAL COLUMN (4) / NUMBER ENTRIES COLUMN (4)	
					REJECTION RATE	
					DIVIDE:	
					COLUMN 7 TOTAL / COLUMN 6 TOTAL	

the number of rejects will be zero, reducing the primary information requirements to items 1, 2, 3, 6, and 7. Since in order to purge your open-order files you would have to review the order anyway, this process simply adds a structure and documentation activity to this purge.

From this purchase-order review, as is evident from the above information, you will be collecting data pertaining to delivery, freight, and total business in dollars conducted with each of your significant vendors and entering this information to the "Vendor-Performance Data-Collection Form."

CLAIMS DATA COLLECTION. Along with these data, it is also necessary to provide vendor claim information. Recording the claims information required by this form will require almost no time in comparison to the above. This minimal time requirement is largely due to the fact that few total orders will have outstanding claims, but is also dependent on establishing a claim routing system through your department so that an order-claims search is unnecessary. If your clerical personnel are forced to search each order for claims information, the collection time will increase; but if you identify one person in each of your buying sections as your claims coordinator, through whom all claims flow both to the buyer and to your accounting department, columns 13, 14, and 15 can be recorded for your significant vendors by this individual without a special search.

COST-IMPROVEMENT DATA COLLECTION. The time required for collecting cost-improvement contribution information is also minimal, since in accordance with the recommendation below you will simply be transcribing summary information submitted by your vendors.

Two alternatives for data collection are available for this information. One of these collects information from the type of cost-reduction reporting program suggested in Chapter 5. The other requests vendors to identify and report their own cost-reduction contributions.

Under the purchasing cost-reduction reporting system, the buyer has the responsibility to credit a vendor for a contribution by referencing the contributing vendor's name on his cost-reduction docket prior to submittal. To receive credit for a cost-reduction contribution, the vendor would have to initiate and/or play a key role in the cost improvement.

The vendor-reporting system, unlike the above system, places both the burden of identification and the clerical job of tabulating contributions on the vendor. Under this system the buyer's review of the vendor's report will serve as the audit to assure that the savings and activities reported are justified. This method could be initiated very simply in the form of a notification letter and procedure akin to that referenced in Appendix 2.

In addition to reducing the clerical burden, this method has two advantages over buyer reporting. One is that the vendor can have no complaints as to the fairness of the cost-improvement total reported since he is responsible for this identification. Secondly, the necessity for vendor reporting at regular intervals serves as a prod to constantly reinforce the intent and purpose of your program (cost improvement). For these reasons the vendor-reporting system, referenced in Appendix 2, is recommended as the preferred data-collection method.

With implementation of this procedure, obtaining and transcribing this information necessitates only initiating the procedure described in Appendix 2, receiving vendor cost-contribution submittals, and transcribing this vendor information to the data-collection form in column 19.

As with claims, the time required for this activity is insignificant compared to the purchase-order collection.

Data Manipulation

On implementation of this collection procedure, you will have available all of the data required to provide the structure for efficient vendor selection and expediting. However, prior to using this data, one more step is required. This consists of preparing the data and displaying the result for each significant vendor in a form convenient to buyer use. This process is summarized on the collection form in columns 11, 17, and 20, but a more detailed review of the procedure that documents these steps should be valuable to an understanding of the total system.

As with the data-collection system, this procedure has been designed so that it can be implemented at a minimum expense. These data can be fully prepared on a quarterly basis as described below, assuming the average number of orders per significant vendor is 5, for only 6 hours per quarter or 2 hours per month in a department handling 15,000 orders per year.

Valuation

The first step in the procedure is data valuation. Once you have collected the measures described with respect to the hidden-cost factors, it is then necessary to value their cost effect before you use them in expediting or vendor-selection decisions. The valuation techniques that follow have been simplified for manual application through the use of averaging and pretabled computation methods.

If you have this information on the computer, you may prefer to apply the formulae contained in the Appendixes to value these costs. These formulae will yield more precise results but are overly time-consuming with respect to the benefit available if you must value this data manually.

EARLY-SHIPMENT EVALUATION. The information pertaining to the cost of early shipment is contained in columns 5 (weeks early) and 9 (total shipment value) on the data-collection form.

For ease of valuation, transfer the entries in column 9 that correspond to early shipments to column 8 (early shipment value) and follow the procedure below for each vendor costing. Remember this will not have to be done for every vendor since few will be registering early shipments.

1. Total column 5 values to find *total weeks early*.
2. Divide the column 5 total by the number of entries in column 5 to find *average time early*.

3. Total the column 8 values to find *total dollars received early* from each vendor.

4. Apply Table 3 to value the cost contribution of these early shipments.

To apply table:

1. Find column 2 answer (early-shipment $ multiplier) corresponding to vendor's average weeks early.

2. Multiply column 2 answer by total value of early shipment for vendor to value cost.

By applying this procedure and the table above, you can quickly and easily compute the early-shipment cost for each of your vendors without having to proceed through the relatively complex formula referenced in Appendix 3.

CLAIMS-COST VALUATION. The claims-cost valuation method is very similar to that for early shipment. The information pertaining to claims cost is contained in columns 13, 14, and 15. The first step in claims valuation is to identify the number of weeks that the claim has been outstanding and record this period in column 16. This period is obtained by subtracting the date in column 14 from that in column 15 (if 15 is blank, enter the current date and perform the above subtraction). Next:

1. Compute *total weeks* in column 16 by adding all entries on each vendor.

2. Divide total weeks by number of entries in column 16 to compute *average weeks outstanding*.

3. Compute total for entries in column 13 to identify *total claim value outstanding*.

4. Apply Table 4 to identify claims cost per vendor.

To apply table:

1. Find column 2 answer (claim cost factor) corresponding to vendor's average weeks early.

2. Multiply column 2 answer by total value of outstanding claims to value claims cost.

Again, by following this procedure and applying this table, you avoid the necessity of using a detailed formula to compute the claims cost.

TABLE 3. Valuation Early Shipment[1]

Average Number Weeks Early	Early-Shipment[2] $ Multiplier
1	0.00212
2	0.00423
3	0.00634
4	0.00846
5	0.01050
6	0.01269
7	0.01470
8	0.01692
9	0.01904
10	0.02115

[1] For derivation, justification and table cost modification method, refer to Appendix 3.
[2] Based on 11 percent; interest, insurance, and tax charges.

TABLE 4. Claim Cost Factors @ 8% Borrowing Cost

Weeks Outstanding	Claim Cost[1] Factor
1	0.0015
2	0.0030
3	0.0045
4	0.0060
5	0.0075
6	0.0090
7	0.0105
8	0.0120
9	0.0135
10	0.0150

[1] For definition, justification and table cost modification method, refer to Appendix 4.

LEADTIME AND LATE-DELIVERY COST VALUATION.   It is also possible to convert a vendor's late-delivery characteristics into a cost contribution, as was done for early shipment and claims. Methods to accomplish this conversion are discussed in Appendix 5. Briefly, the method described in this Appendix identifies the cost of your vendor's quoted leadtime in terms of inventory required to support that leadtime, and the cost of unreliable delivery based on an approximation of the inventory necessary to prevent a stock-out resulting from the identified unreliability level.

As you will note, however, this approximation will be suitable only for material which is ordered repetitively; you will not be able to back up or protect sporadic requirements if you cannot predict the demand. Further, since application of these techniques requires that a buyer have knowledge of the applicable inventory order-review point and safety-stock relationships of his major stocked materials, without a computerized assist this approach can be very time-consuming. Therefore, it is suggested that this quantification be conducted only on an exception basis, described later in the vendor-selection application, unless you can computerize the process and your purchases are primarily for inventoried material.

Regardless of whether you choose to quantify on an exception or total basis, we do have the necessary data secured in the information on the collection form. As was discussed, the characteristics of late delivery that contribute to cost are the number of days overdue and the frequency of late delivery or, in other words, the total delivery delay. For purposes of analysis, four summary pieces of information are necessary and may be identified from the collection form by following the procedure below:

1. *Compute Total Delivery Delay.* Total the entries in column 4 to obtain this measure.
2. *Compute Average Period Overdue.* Divide the total delivery delay by the number of entries in column 4.
3. *Compute Percentage Overdue.* Divide number of entries in column 4 by number of entries in column 1.
4. *Compute Percentage Overdue Contributed by Quality Defects.* Divide number of entries in column 7 by number of entries in column 6.

In this information you have displayed the past probability that a vendor's delivery will not meet his promise date (percentage overdue), the magnitude of the delay to be expected (average period overdue), and the percentage of these overdues contributed by quality defects rather than scheduling or processing errors (percentage quality defects). In effect you have profiled the vendor's past delivery history. The next section will describe the application method for this information in vendor selection and expediting.

FREIGHT AND COST-IMPROVEMENT CONTRIBUTION. The final hidden cost factors, freight and cost-improvement contribution costs, are also available from the collection form. In column 10 you have recorded all of the freight bills received from each vendor. Totaling this column results in the total freight bill paid to the vendor under review.

The cost-improvement contribution is also already valued, and is referenced in column 19 on the data-collection form.

Common Denominator

Once you have valued the hidden-cost factors as described, it is necessary to complete the final step in data manipulation, creation of a common denominator and summation of all these cost factors in order to provide an analysis format convenient to the buyer's use.

A common denominator is necessary to pull all of these cost factors together, especially in vendor selection. We need a factor that converts the historical costs related to freight, quality, cost improvement, and delivery to a common basis with respect to price and terms of payment. In effect, we must relate these historical costs to the elements of each quotation that would be received from a vendor: price, terms of payment, and leadtime. Starting from the basis of price minus terms of payment, you, in effect, are interested in knowing what additional costs are involved in doing business with a vendor. In other words, you must identify how these hidden costs have been historically related to price. This relationship can be provided by totaling the hidden costs collected for each vendor and dividing by the dollars purchased or received from that vendor over the same time span (recorded in column 9 on collection form).

$$\text{Hidden Cost Ratio} = \frac{(\text{Freight Cost}) + (\text{Claims Cost}) + (\text{Early-Shipment Cost}) - (\text{Cost-Improvement Contribution})}{(\$ \text{ Purchased})}$$

With this relationship you are, in effect, expressing the additional costs incurred for each dollar invested with that vendor. For example, assume your cost factors for a vendor were:

1. Freight = $100,000
2. Claims Cost = $20,000
3. Early-Shipment Cost = $10,000
4. Cost-Improvement Contribution = $70,000
5. $ Purchased = $1,000,000

You would know that historically for each dollar you paid in price you have also paid six cents in terms of the other costs. This is computed as follows:

$$\text{Hidden Cost Factor} = \frac{(\$100,000) + (\$20,000) + (\$10,000) - (\$70,000)}{(\$1,000,000)} = .06$$

Consequently, it is reasonable to assume that the cost of doing business with this vendor is $1.06 per $1.00 quoted price. In terms of a procedure, this process could be expressed as follows:

1. Sum the costs of freight, early shipment, claims.
2. Subtract from this total the cost-improvement contribution submitted by the vendor.
3. Divide by total dollars purchased (column 9) to identify the cost adders.

If you have opted to quantify the cost of leadtime and late delivery, these two costs should be treated in the identical manner as the above costs. They simply become two additional cost adders to price. If you have not pursued this quantification, leadtime and late delivery will be evaluated in conjunction with but separate from the above cost elements, and therefore will not require the common denominator.

APPLICATION — VENDOR SELECTION: EXPEDITING

To this point we have identified methods for collection and preparation of information pertaining to the "hidden" costs: freight, quality, delivery, and cost-improvement contribution. We have also identified a method for estimating the net savings resulting from a terms-of-payment offer. As you will recall, the objective of this section was stated as to provide the information and techniques necessary to efficient total material-related-cost decisionmaking in vendor selection and expediting prioritization. We now have all the information collected and prepared to enable us to describe a technique to accomplish this objective.

Vendor-Selection Procedure

After a common demoninator has been established and you have computed the hidden-cost ratio for each of your significant vendors, you will be able to apply the following vendor-selection procedure. The first step in this procedure consists of using the hidden-cost ratio to compute the net cost associated with a vendor's proposal. This process can be depicted as follows:

$$\text{Net cost} = \text{Price} - (\text{Price})(NT) + \text{Price (Hidden Cost Ratio)}$$

where:

> NT = Net terms of payment as found through application of Tables 1 and 2.

> Price (Hidden-Cost Ratio) = The price adder as determined by the composition of the historical:

> 1. Freight
> 2. Early shipment
> 3. Claims
> 4. Minus cost-improvement contribution costs

When you provide a buyer with the hidden-cost ratio rather than the separate elements of this ratio, he is required to work with only three factors in valuing proposals: the price, net terms of payment, and this hidden-cost ratio. Consequently, only price, freight, and terms need be considered, as in the "visible"-cost valuation.

Further, if you have opted to include the quantified cost of leadtime and late delivery in this ratio as well as the above costs, this net-cost computation alone will identify your lowest-total-cost vendor. If, instead, you have chosen to quantify these characteristics only as an exception basis as suggested in our discussion, the additional step described below is necessary in your vendor-selection procedure.

This vendor-selection technique identifies the "expected delivery" for each vendor through the use of probabilities. It is this technique that in the absence of a sophisticated computer program appears to be most suitable to valuing delivery characteristics.

In attempting to identify the expected delivery, it is necessary to relate the quoted leadtime to the probability of an order being overdue and the average period overdue. This process and its decision application in vendor selection may be summarized as follows:

1. Add the product of the average time overdue and the percentage overdue to the quoted leadtimes of each vendor.

   $$LT_E = LT + ((OD)(\%OD))$$

   where:

LT = Quoted leadtime in weeks
OD = Average overdue period in weeks
$\%OD$ = Percentage of overdue orders
LT_E = Expected leadtime

This calculation provides an "expected" leadtime for each vendor taking into account not only their promise but also reliability of delivery performance.

2. If the expected leadtime for the lowest-cost vendor (other than delivery) is the lowest, this vendor should receive the order.

3. If the expected leadtime for the lowest-cost vendor is higher, clear your decision with the department responsible for production planning by asking, "Will a cost greater than the potential savings available be expended due to the longer delivery?" or, if the order is for stock material, refer to Appendix 5 to identify the associated stock-out prevention cost of each offer.

In implementing this procedure, you will find it helpful to use the following "Bid-Analysis Form" which not only summarizes this approach and provides a vendor-selection worksheet, but also serves as an award-justification form to document the selection criteria for your purchase-order files.

To illustrate the use of this form and to summarize this vendor-selection process, let us assume that we have received three vendor quotations containing the following:

Vendor Quotations

| | | | Terms of Payment | | |
Vendor	Price	Freight	Payment Delay	Progress Payment	Leadtime
Vendor A	$12.00	Not Allowed	Net 60	20%—100 days 30%— 50 days	20 Weeks
Vendor B	$11.00	Not Allowed	2% 10 Net 30	10%—100 days 60%— 40 days	24 Weeks
Vendor C	$13.00	Not Allowed	1% 10 Prox. Net 30	No Progress Payments	22 Weeks

After a review of the historical hidden-cost factors and delivery information obtained from the "Vendor Performance Data-Collection Form," we have also found that the following performance factors are applicable for each vendor.

FORM 2. Bid-Analysis Form

	1	2	3	4	5	6	7	8	9	10
				Terms of Payment Savings (use decimal)	Cost Ratio (3–4)	Terms & Hidden Cost (5 × 1)	Net Cost (1 + 2 + 6)		Average Delivery Delay	Expected Delivery (8 + 9)
Vendor (Circle the one selected)	Price	Freight (use only if firm quote)	Hidden Cost Ratio					Lead Time		

Order Value _____

Purchase Order Number _____

Required Date _____

Contract Number _____

Selection Criteria (check)
1. ☐ Lowest net cost & acceptance delivery
2. ☐☐ Delivery: Authorized by _____
3. ☐ Other (Explain) _____
_____
_____

Buyer _____   Date _____

41

Performance Factors

Vendor	Hidden-Cost Factor	Average Delivery Delay
Vendor A	0.06	4 Weeks
Vendor B	0.10	2 Weeks
Vendor C	−0.09	—

The first step in using this form is to value "Terms of Payment" for each vendor. By referring to Tables 1 and 2, we can value these as follows.[1]

Values of Terms of Payment

Vendor	Terms of Payment				Savings Total (1–4)
	1 Discount and Payment Delay	2 Savings[1]	3 Progress Payment	4 Cost[2]	
Vendor A	Net 60	0.017	20%–100 Days	0.0056	
			30%– 50 Days	0.0042	0.007
Vendor B	2% 10 Net 30	0.023	10%–100 Days	0.0028	
			60%– 40 Days	0.0066	0.014
Vendor C	1% 10 Prox. Net 30	0.017	—	0	0.017

[1] From Table 1 and associated procedure.
[2] From Table 2 and associated procedure.

Once terms of payment are valued, you have all the information necessary to select the vendor on the basis of total cost by simply completing the Bid-Analysis Form as instructed and following the steps indicated by the column headings as has been done in Figure 4.

As you can see, even though Vendor B quoted $2.00/unit less than Vendor C, Vendor C provides the greatest value because, historically, he has contributed more in cost savings (reason for negative hidden-cost ratio) and provides a greater savings in terms-of-payment than does Vendor B. Further, Vendor C's expected delivery does not jeopardize the required date. However, if Vendor B's proposal had resulted in the lowest net cost, since it does threaten the required date, it would have been necessary to review these results with your schedulers to determine if the potential late delivery could be justified by the cost savings. If it

[1] This illustration has been intentionally complicated by the inclusion of progress payments in order to provide a comprehensive example. However, recognize that only your largest-value purchases will require this step.

FIGURE 4. Bid Analysis Form Application

Vendor (Circle the one selected)	1 Price	2 Freight (use only if firm quote)	3 Hidden Cost Ratio	4 Terms of Payment Savings (use decimal)	5 Cost Ratio (3–4)	6 Terms and Hidden Cost (5 × 1)	7 Net Cost (1 + 2 + 6)	8 Lead Time	9 Average Delivery Delay	10 Expected Delivery (8 + 9)
Vendor A	12.00	—*	0.06	0.007	0.053	0.64	12.64	20	4	24
Vendor B	11.00	—	0.10	0.014	0.086	0.95	11.95	24	2	26
Vendor C	13.00	—	-0.09	0.017	-.107	-1.39	11.61	22	0	22

Purchase Order Number 89704
Contract Number 55669203

Order Value $8,000
Required Date 25 weeks

Selection Criteria (check)

1. ☑ Lowest net cost & acceptance delivery
2. ☐ Lowest Net Cost With Acceptable Delivery: Authorized by ___
3. ☐ Other (Explain). Use if performance or other factors reverse above direction.

Buyer M.C. Johns   Date 5/7/74

*Leave blank since freight has not been quoted firm by vendor.

could not, you would be forced to select the next-lowest-cost vendor and check block 2 in the "Selection Criteria" section of this form.

Expediting Procedure

With two of these same measures, number of orders late and overdue period, recorded on a historical basis for your vendors, it is also possible to structure your expediting attack on the basis of which vendors will contribute the greatest potential delivery delay for your department. Unlike the vendor-selection application, this expediting technique uses "raw data" in steering your attack. This is because in attempting to improve delivery performance for your department through expediting, the most significant improvement will result from concentrating on the vendors who cause the greatest total-delivery delays. Percentages used for this purpose can hide and distort the vendor's significance to department performance. For illustration purposes, late-delivery indexes for two vendors, one shipping 10 orders with 1 overdue and the other shipping 100 orders with 10 overdue, would be identical at 10 percent. However, if the vendor shipping 10 orders late was an average of 5 weeks overdue, he has caused 50 weeks of delays. Even if the other vendor has 10 weeks overdue on his one order, he has only caused 10 weeks of delays. Clearly, the vendor causing the greatest problem would be the one contributing the greatest number of "weeks delivery delay," not necessarily the vendor having the greatest overdue rate or average time overdue.

As a result of this conclusion, late-delivery information should be displayed as in Form 3 with the vendors listed in rank order of greatest delivery-delay contribution.

FORM 3. Significant Vendors (Late Delivery)[1]

	Delivery Delay	Number of Late Deliveries	Average Time Overdue	Orders Late Due to Rejections	Shipment-Rejection Rate	Late-Delivery Index
Vendor A	500	50	10 Wks.	30	60%	50%
Vendor B	480	40	12	25	50%	40%
Vendor C	360	45	8	20	50%	45%
Vendor D	120	8	15	4	50%	80%

[1] All of this information is available in Form 1.

There are two basic applications for this information. One enables you to select the correct "expediting mode" for any particular order. The other identifies how to proceed to efficiently reduce the total delivery delays that you have experienced.

Mode of Expediting

In determining the proper mode of expediting for any particular order, it is important to realize that three basic options can be applied: exception expediting, routine status check, and advance expediting.

Exception expediting is the most typical method applied by purchasing departments. This consists of calling a vendor to obtain a revised promise date only after the original promise date has been missed. The method involving a routine status check is much more time-consuming but prevents unpleasant surprises. Application of this method necessitates calling vendors at preset intervals so that you are able to inform your shop of schedule delays at the earliest possible moment, and can offer an opportunity for working around the late delivery rather than suffering through it.

The third expediting method, advance expediting, is the most time-consuming of all; it attempts to assure supply instead of just providing warning of a late delivery. This method consists of using milestone, critical path, or similar scheduling techniques that identify critical steps in your vendor's manufacturing process, and thus enable you to review progress against these schedules. This identifies potential delays and allows you to take necessary corrective action to insure timely delivery.

For example, if you asked your vendor to break down his leadtime into activities (manufacturing and processing steps), identifying the earliest initiation and anticipated completion date for each, the latest possible dates for initiation and completion to uphold the schedule, and the sequence of these activities, you would have a ready tool for spotting critical activities and potential delays as you proceeded through the manufacturing cycle. You would also have early notification and be able to assure that corrective action is taken for any observed delay. This process has been depicted graphically in Figure 5. As should be evident, however, this expediting process is the most costly and must be applied only in your most critical areas.

The key to efficient application of these three techniques is to provide a simple means of identifying which one is applicable to any particular order. This can be done by obtaining a list of your critical commodities[1] and combining this list with a list of your unreliable vendors (those contributing the most delivery delays). By combining these two lists on Form 4 and classifying entries in the manner that will be discussed, you can readily provide an expediting plan for your buyers.

The rationale behind the classification in Column 3 can be stated as follows. If a vendor has historically been reliable in delivery, you should only expedite where you have indications that you are in trouble (excep-

[1]Defined as those commodities that set your manufacturing schedule (as in Figure 5). Obtain this from your scheduling department.

1. Identify the *time required* to complete each major processing activity (A, B, C, etc.) and *sequence of* activities.

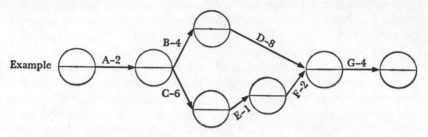

2. Identify the *earliest start and finish* times for each activity by adding consecutive activity times (starting with A) and placing answers in the upper portion of each activity circle.

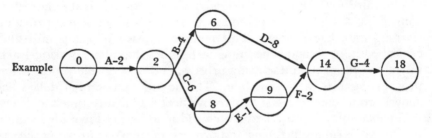

3. Identify *latest start and finish* times by subtracting consecutive activity times (working back from G) and placing answers in the lower portion of each activity circle.

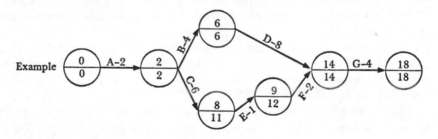

4. The *critical path* is identified by those activities for which there is no "slack" (difference between earliest and latest start and finish times).

FIGURE 5.   Critical Path Identification

tion expediting). Otherwise you will be creating needless administrative expense for yourself and for the vendor, who in all probability will deliver on time anyway.

The status-check method should be designated only for those orders placed with vendors who have contributed significant delivery delays in

FORM 4. Commodity-Vendor Expediting Classification Form

Name of Significant Late-Delivery Vendor	Critical Commodities Supplied	Expediting Classification
Vendor A	None	Status Check
Vendor C	Motors	Advance Expediting
Vendor E	Structural Steel	Advance Expediting
Vendor Z	None	Status Check
All Others	None	Exception Only

the past, but who do not supply critical commodities. Since the commodities are not classified as critical, some schedule slip can be tolerated. Consequently, the aim is to keep in contact with the vendor to identify schedule slip at the earliest possible moment. This will enable your shop either to make necessary adjustments in their plans or to advise that advance expediting is now required since this commodity, due to slippage, has become critical.

Finally, if the vendor is unreliable and the commodity critical, advance expediting is called for, and the buyer should apply milestone or critical-path techniques to assure supply. Once you have compiled this list and instructed your buyers in its use, you will also find it worthwhile to provide color-coded tabs for each classification to simplify expediting from your order file.

DELIVERY-DELAY REDUCTION. The preceding application will enable you to establish an efficient daily expediting program. However, it is also important to work to reduce vendor unreliability, in order to produce a comparable reduction in the need for applying the more time-consuming expediting techniques. Again, we can use the results from Form 3, "Significant Vendors (Late Delivery)," in order to identify the vendors of most importance to this effort. Once these vendors are identified, you can use the quality-related information that was collected on this form to establish a delivery-delay reduction attack as follows:

I. Using the "Vendor Delivery-Delay List," identify those 10 percent of vendors who contributed 80 percent of your section's delivery delays. For these, determine whether they fall under A or B below, apply, and proceed as instructed.
   A. If quality deficiency is the vendor's major cause for delays, identify if other vendors producing similar commodities also have a high frequency of quality deficiencies.

1. If they do, plan to reduce this delay through applica-
    tion of the "Design-Redesign" Procedure in Chapter 5.
2. If they do not, plan to reduce this delay through
    a. Identifying what this vendor does differently and
        modifying his processing procedure; or
    b. If this is not feasible due to vendor refusal to
        change and economics of doing business with this
        vendor, apply "Design-Redesign" Procedure in
        Chapter 5.

B. If scheduling deficiency is the vendor's major cause for de-
    lay, identify if other vendors producing similar com-
    modities also have a high frequency of scheduling deficien-
    cies.
    1. If they do, plan to reduce this delay through application
        of the "Contracting" Procedure in Chapter 5.
    2. If they do not, plan to reduce this delay through
        a. Identifying what this vendor does differently and
            modifying his scheduling procedure; or
        b. If this is not possible due to vendor refusal to
            change and economics of doing business with this
            vendor, apply "Contracting" Procedure in Chapter
            5.
C. Through the above analysis, develop a delivery-im-
    provement plan and report progress against plan monthly.

In this manner you can establish a delivery-delay reduction program
that identifies and attacks the cause for the problem rather than simply
accepting a vendor's poor delivery performance.

SUMMARY

This chapter has identified methods enabling display of material-
related costs in a form convenient to a buyer's use for vendor selection
and expediting. The material-related costs and cost influences requiring
analysis were identified as: Terms of payment, Freight, Early-shipment
cost, Cost-improvement contribution, Claims cost, Costs related to late
delivery, and Costs related to leadtime.

A method was identified to structure your expediting attack based on
those vendors contributing the greatest number of delivery delays
and/or those contributing the greatest magnitude of late-delivery cost
(described in Appendix 5 for stock material).

The vendor-selection technique that was proposed summarized the above costs into one index related to price. This index was then used in conjunction with price in order to display net cost as follows: Net Cost = Price (Price (Net Discount)) + (Hidden-Cost Price Ratio).

The intent of this application was to provide no more application complexity than the buyer encounters in computing the more limited version of net cost using just the visible cost factors of: (Price) + (Freight) − (Price)(Discount).

In the absence of buying primarily for stocked or inventoried material, an expected-delivery depiction was also suggested for use in vendor selection. This measure combined the quoted leadtime with the probable delivery delay from each vendor to assist in assessing which vendor offered greater assurance of supply. The expression was depicted as follows: Expected Delivery = (Leadtime) + ((% Overdue) × (Average Time Overdue)).

In conjunction with this depiction it was recommended that you:

1. Select the lowest-net-cost vendor if expected delivery is also lowest or if expected delivery falls within required leadtime.
2. Review cost of doing business with lowest-net-cost vendor if expected delivery does not meet above conditions. Review with production control and/or compute quality-protection cost as in Appendix 5 if material is for stock.

An information-collection device and procedure was reviewed that allows collection and depiction of this information for a department with 15,000 orders per year with only a six-hour clerical effort per month.

Besides allowing you to make and justify better vendor-selection and expediting decisions, these techniques have one further significant benefit. In acquainting your vendors with your selection techniques, you are emphasizing your objectives and providing incentive for improved vendor performance. It is one thing to tell a vendor that his delivery is bad and must be improved, but significantly plainer to tell him that he lost an order due to unacceptable delivery reliability and point out this fact with numbers. The incentive to improve cost-reduction contribution, delivery reliability, and quality is also significantly greater when included in a formal vendor-selection application.

Efforts have been made throughout this chapter to simplify depiction, collection, and analysis of these costs. Undoubtedly there is a clerical price to pay for this effort, but the investment will be well spent in professionalizing your decisionmaking and vendor awareness of significant performance as related to cost.

=3

Routine Improvement Activities

Engaging in routine improvement activities involves very little application time in addition to that required for performing maintenance duties but significantly extends the scope and cost effectiveness of purchasing. These activities can be grouped as follows: combining or splitting requisitions, escalation hedging, quantity-break procurement, elimination of requisitions, and routine new source development.

These activities can and should be pursued in conjunction with a buyer's daily duties. Such pursuit can be easily justified by the available return. The potential cost savings are great; and yet, the time required to identify an opportunity for application and to determine the course of action is minimal. As you will see, this guaranteed yield situation is a result of decision-making techniques that have been developed for identifying routine improvement opportunities through normal vendor contact and quickly and easily determining if you should capitalize on these opportunities.

Without these decision-making techniques, application of the improvement activities can be very complex and time-consuming since there are a number of variables involved with each. To illustrate this point, consider the requirements of effective routine improvement decisions. Vendor or market knowledge is needed for review of your own past decisions or those made by other departments concerning the most economical method of fulfilling your material needs. Combining or splitting of requisitions requires questioning the mode of ordering; escalation hedging requires questioning the timing of the order; quantity-break buying requires questioning the efficient ordering quantity; elimination of an order requires questioning the necessity of the order;

and new source development requires expanding the choices available in maintenance and expediting decisions. Costs justify whether your present method or an alternate one is the most efficient. It is this costing process that is most difficult, for in each of the routine improvement activities, your decisions will involve at least three offsetting costs: price, inventory, and purchase order clerical costs. If these costs are not properly depicted and applied your decisions will be contrary to your lowest material-related cost objective.

However, with the following decision-making techniques you can overcome this difficulty and facilitate the total application process. You will be able to structure this questioning process, from the identification of a possible application, through the costing of alternatives, to making your decision based on the most favorable cost outcome. Let us first investigate the activity of combining and splitting requisitions.

COMBINING AND SPLITTING REQUISITIONS

Opportunities for combining or splitting requisitions can be identified very easily as you proceed through your normal review of unplaced requisitions. The identification method and decision-making approach for this activity are described below.

Combining Requisitions

The opportunity for combining requisitions — merging two or more into one — is present whenever material requirements on more than one requisition are capable of being supplied by one vendor.

If required dates on these requisitions are similar, combination should definitely be pursued. You will incur only a minimal rewriting cost and will save the cost associated with handling additional purchase orders.[1] In conjunction with the clerical cost savings available through combination, additional savings will often be provided in the price of the material as a result of the efficiency you provide the vendor by reducing his paperwork and increasing his production flexibility.

If required dates are dissimilar, combination can still be investigated, but this investigation must be well structured. You will be able to identify your lowest-cost ordering alternative by requesting quotations on each requisition requirement individually, on receiving award of total re-

[1]Methods for valuing purchase order processing savings are included in Appendix 7.

quirement (delivered in accordance with specified required dates), and on the total requirement shipped at one time.

The first alternative will reveal the base cost for ordering in accordance with "as requisitioned" instructions. The second displays the price benefit, if any, that the vendor will offer for the guarantee of receiving the total lot of material. The third alternative offers the vendor the greatest potential cost savings in terms of production, transportation, and storage efficiency and, consequently, offers you the greatest opportunity for price reduction. It also offers the opportunity of obtaining an order-processing savings in that consolidation into one purchase order is beneficial due to the single shipment aspect implicit in this option. Alternatives one and two do not offer this processing benefit since individual shipments must still be processed and the costs must still be incurred for this processing. However, the drawback to alternative three is that it will require that you incur inventory charges prior to the use of that portion of material received in advance of the requisition required date.

Selection between alternatives one and two should be based on a lowest total-net-cost analysis as described in Chapter 2. However, if alternative three appears the most attractive, it is necessary to extend this analysis by applying the quantity-break decision rules that will be presented later in this chapter since you must justify the accompanying inventory investment.

Splitting Requisitions

Splitting a requisition into two or more should be pursued only when the potential cost advantages are great enough to offset the additional purchase order processing costs that will be incurred. There are two typical situations in which the splitting opportunity could be advantageous: First, if the commodity mix on the order cannot efficiently be handled by one vendor, in which case identification of the situation can be achieved by reviewing item costs on competitive quotes or comparing item price histories to quoted item prices; and second, if some of the items on the order have very short leadtimes and require a premium price to guarantee receipt whereas shipment of other items could be delayed enabling placement with other than a premium price vendor, in which case identification of the situation can proceed through a review of required dates and corresponding quotations or price histories.

To value the potential savings available from splitting, subtract the additional purchase order processing cost incurred (the order-issuance cost times the number of additional purchase orders issued) from the price or transportation advantage received. If this computation indicates that a savings is possible, the split is justified.

EXTENDED PROCUREMENT

Quantity-breaks and price increases can also present opportunities for obtaining cost improvement. Potential quantity-break information can be requested as you attempt to price your requisitions, and a decision reached concerning the optimum quantity prior to order placement. Potential price-hedging gains will exist with each price escalation and notification of the escalation will serve to initiate your price-hedging activity.

Quantity-break and escalation-hedge procurement present a much more complicated application than that required to combine or split requisitions. However, the potential cost advantages are also much greater. It has long been recognized that there are cost advantages available through extended procurement, but identifying specifically how much additional material should be procured is extremely complex.

Significant attempts have been made by others to provide tools that simplify these decisions. Unfortunately, these tools have not been completely effective; and, even with their aid, many attempts at advance procurement still result in losses or missed opportunities. The application difficulty associated with existing methods is summarized below:

1. Difficulty in identifying the available savings due to:
    a. Inadequate cost analysis
        1) Use of unsuitable costing methods
        2) Lack of cost-influence visibility
    b. Difficulty in applying existing decision-making techniques due to:
        1) Intimidating appearance
        2) Lack of simple method to modify existing systems for cost other than those used in examples
2. Failure to consider resulting inventory increases as investments to be justified by return on investment analysis.

The following techniques and procedures have been designed to overcome these problems by describing a system that enables easy determination of the optimizing quantity-break/escalation-hedge decisions while assuring that decisions reached are consistent with your company's financial objectives. Appendix 6 includes information that enables you to apply these procedures to your operation.

The procedures below are manual systems that you can apply without the aid of a computer. Alternate, computerized techniques are also available and, in fact, the formulae presented in Appendix 6 may be used to obtain these same results from computer application. However, a manual system is still necessary since the cost associated with these computerized techniques is difficult to justify except in the largest divisions or companies. Even for those who can provide this justification, it is desirable to have these manual tools available to aid in the buyer's understanding and to enable him to make decisions in situations in which computer assistance is not readily available.

Escalation Hedging

In escalation hedging it is necessary to identify the maximum quantity of material that can be procured in advance of its normal required date and prior to an expected price increase in order to provide the desired return on investment. Obviously, the first step in making this determination must be the identification of the magnitude and timing of the expected price increase. There are any number of methods by which this may be accomplished. The most common are review of published information, negotiating to assure vendor notification in sufficient time to react prior to the increase, and requesting forecasting assistance through application of techniques that will be discussed in Chapter 4.

For example, assume that you have applied one of these methods and have discovered that a 9 percent price increase is expected on December 31. With this information you will proceed as follows:

I. Determine the maximum quantity of material that you can justify hedging based on your expected price increase. To make this determination, apply Escalation Hedge Tables as follows:

   A. Refer to column 1 in the table and locate the number nearest to your expected escalation.

   In this example, 9.2 percent in column 1 most closely corresponds to the expected 9.0 percent increase and thus row 5 is applicable to this decision.

   B. Refer across the row identified above to column 2 in order to find the maximum hedge in months that can be supported by this escalation.

   In this example since row 5 was identified, the maximum hedge as found in column 2 of the table is a five-month supply of material.

TABLE 5. Escalation Hedge[1]

Percentage of Anticipated[2] Price Increase (% P)	Hedge (in Months) (N)	Percentage of Expected Savings[3]
1.8	1	0.6
3.7	2	1.8
5.5	3	3.0
7.3	4	4.2
9.2	5	5.4
11.0	6	6.6
12.8	7	7.8
14.6	8	9.0
16.5	9	10.2
18.3	10	11.4
20.0	11	12.6
22.0	12	13.9

[1] Table derivation documented in Appendix 6.
[2] Computed using Minimal Acceptable Yield = %ROI (15%) + Insurance & Taxes (7%)
[3] Computed using Inventory Cost = Borrowing Cost (8%) + Insurance & Taxes (7%)

II. Determine if less than this maximum hedge should be procured through a review of obsolescence, deterioration, and space availability considerations as follows:

A. Identify which of the factors below, if any, will restrict the amount of hedge. Proceed as instructed.

1. Obsolescence review

   If obsolescence of the material will occur prior to the use of the maximum hedge, reduce this hedge to a quantity that will not become obsolete.

2. Deterioration review

   If deterioration is a factor, estimate the expected percentage of value lost per month.

   a. Deduct this percentage deterioration from the expected escalation. In this example, if we assume that 2 percent will be lost per month, we would deduct this 2 percent from the 9 percent expected escalation to arrive at a 7 percent remainder.
   b. Find this remainder in column 1 of the table and refer to column 2 to identify the adjusted hedge recommendation.

In this example, the 7 percent remainder would be most closely approximated by the 7.3 percent referenced in row 4 of column 1. Thus, deterioration would result in reducing the hedge recommendation from five months to the four months referenced in column 2 of this row.

3. Space review

   a. If space is available that will not be used for the term of the hedge in an alternate activity yielding greater than the necessary return on investment, you should not further reduce the recommended hedge.

   b. If space is not available, reduce the hedge to correspond to available space.

     For example, assume that you find that space is available for only a three-month hedge.

B. Identify which of the above factors presents the greatest restriction on the amount of material to be hedged to determine your hedging recommendation.

   1. If none of these factors has restricted quantity, you are advised to hedge the maximum amount.

   2. If there are restrictions, you are advised to hedge in accordance with the greatest restriction.

     In this example, space presents the greatest restriction (three months). Consequently, hedge only this three-month quantity.

III. Advise your requisitioners to issue requisitions and/or order-change notices in accordance with your hedge recommendation.

     In this example, you would advise the requisitioner to order so that a three-month supply of material can be delivered prior to the effective date of the price increase.

Although these few steps are all that are necessary for effective hedge decisionmaking, it is advantageous to include a further step to motivate the buyer. This consists of providing the buyer an efficient means of identifying the dollar savings that he has brought about through hedging so that he can obtain recognition for his efforts. The following procedure provides an efficient method for this savings identification:

I. Cost reduction identification

In order to quickly and easily identify the savings you have obtained through hedging, determine whether A. or B. (below) apply and follow the substeps as directed.

A. If the maximum hedge was procured, value your savings as follows using the Escalation Hedge Table.

1. Your percentage anticipated savings will be referenced in column 3 in the row corresponding to the number of months hedged.

For example, if you had hedged the maximum quantity identified above (five months), the corresponding savings in column 3 is 5.4 percent.

2. To convert this percentage to dollars savings, multiply by the dollar value of material hedged.

B. If less than the maximum hedge was procured, value your savings as follows using the Escalation Hedge Table.

1. Subtract the increase referenced in column 1 corresponding to the actual numbers of months hedged from the expected escalation.

In the above example, due to the space restriction, you were allowed to hedge only three months of material even though the expected increase was 9.0 percent. The increase referenced in column 1 corresponding to the three-month hedge, however, is only 5.5 percent. By performing the above subtraction, we obtain (9.0 percent — 5.5 percent) 3.5 percent.

2. Add this remainder to the expected savings found in column 3 that corresponds to the actual number of months hedged to identify the expected savings.

In this example a 4.0 percent savings (column 3) corresponds to the three months actually hedged. Consequently, the total percentage savings is equal to (4.0 percent + 3.5 percent) 7.5 percent.

3. To convert this percentage to dollars, multiply by the total value of material hedged.

This concludes the working portion of the hedging procedure. However, this whole procedure revolves around the validity of the Escalation Hedge Table and in order to insure effective decisions, it is necessary that this table reflect actual costs. The steps necessary to refine this table for your operation's cost structure are documented in Appendix 6.

Quantity-Break Procedure

Unlike the escalation-hedge situation in which the percentage of price advantage is independent of the specific amount brought in early, the price advantage from the quantity break is entirely dependent on being able to buy the specified quantity. Consequently, the decision amounts to: "Will the return on investment from procuring the additional quantity be sufficient to justify the investment?" In this case you either justify the quantity buy or do not engage in the activity. There is no advantage to cutting back and buying a lesser quantity as in the hedge activity since the price break would not be available at the reduced quantity.

As with the hedge procedure, the first step in initiating a quantity-break investigation must be to identify the opportunities available. Information can be obtained from published price-quantity information, or vendor responses to inquiries that have requested quotations on quantities above and below those authorized for requisition.

Once the potential advantage is identified you must determine if the quantity buy is justified. For example, assume that you have identified the following price advantage:

100-unit price = $1.05/unit (normal order quantity)
150-unit price = $1.00/unit

With this information proceed as follows to identify the minimum acceptable yield:

1. Convert price-break quantity and normal ordering quantity into number-of-months supply of material in order to find price-break months supply and normal months supply. (For inventory items this can be done by dividing each quantity by average usage per month)

    Example: Assume the average usage per month equals 25 units. Therefore, price-break months supply equals 6 months and normal months supply equals 4 months.

2. Determine excess months supply by subtracting the normal months supply from the price-break months supply.

    Example: Excess months supply equals (6 − 4) equals 2 months

3. Refer to the Quantity Break Table (Table 6) and find the

TABLE 6.   Quantity-Break Table[1]

Excess Months Supply (X_e)	Percentage of Minimum Acceptable Yield (%Y)[2]	Percentage of Inventory Cost[3]
1	0.92	0.63
2	1.83	1.26
3	2.75	1.89
4	3.67	2.52
5	4.58	3.15
6	5.50	3.78
7	6.42	4.41
8	7.34	5.04
9	8.25	5.67
10	9.17	6.30
11	10.08	6.93
12	11.00	7.50

[1]Table derivation documented in Appendix 6.
[2]Computed using (Minimal Acceptable Yield) =
  15% (ROI)
  7% (Insurance & Taxes) = 22%
[3]Computed using (Applicable Inventory Cost) =
  8% (Borrowing cost)
  7% (Insurance & Taxes) = 15%

minimum acceptable yield (column 2) corresponding to the number of excess months supply.

Example: Minimum acceptable yield for 2 months excess equals 1.83 percent.

Next, it is necessary to see if the savings available from buying the increased quantities (available yield) is greater than the minimum acceptable yield in order to determine if procurement of the break quantity can be justified.

I.   Find the available yield as follows:
   A.   Identify percentage purchase order savings
      1.   Find purchase order savings in dollars using the following Purchase Order Savings Table.

Purchase order savings in dollars is found at the intersection of the applicable Price-Break Months Supply row and Excess Months Supply column in the table.

Example: Price break months = 6
        Excess months = 2
           Savings = $7 (circled in table)

TABLE 7. Purchase Order Savings Table[1] (in dollars)

Price-Break (X_t) Months Supply	Excess Months Supply (X_e)										
	1	2	3	4	5	6	7	8	9	10	11
12	1	3	4	7	9	13	18	26	39	65	143
11	1	3	5	8	10	16	23	35	60	130	
10	1	3	5	9	13	20	30	52	117		
9	1	4	7	10	16	26	46	104			
8	1	4	8	13	22	39	91				
7	3	5	10	17	33	78					
6	3	⑦	13	26	65						
5	3	9	20	52							
4	4	13	39								
3	7	26									
2	13										

[1]Computed using $13 processing cost. Table derivation documented in Appendix 6.

2. Convert savings to a percentage by dividing purchase order savings by the total value of material that must be ordered to reach the quantity break and multiplying answer by 100.

Example: Purchase-order-processing savings
$$= \$ \ 7$$
Total value of material =
$$\$1.00 \times 150 = \$150$$
$$\text{Percentage of savings} = \frac{7}{150} \times 100 = 4.7\%$$

B. Identify the percentage of price savings:
Divide price savings per unit by the quantity-break price. Convert to a percentage by multiplying by 100.

Example: 100-unit price = 1.05
150-unit price = 1.00
$$\text{Percentage price savings} = \frac{.05}{1.00} = 5\%$$

C. The sum of the percentage price savings and percentage purchase order savings is equal to the available yield.

Example: Available yield = 4.7% + 5.0% = 9.7%

II. If the available yield is greater than the minimal acceptable yield, proceed to next step.
If available yield is not greater, the quantity buy cannot be justified.

Example: Minimal acceptable yield $= 1.83\%$
Available yield $= 9.7\%$

Therefore, continue to next step.

III.   Review obsolescence, space availability, and deterioration as follows:

If losses due to expected deterioration and obsolescence are less than the available yield minus the minimal acceptable yield and if space is available to store the material, the quantity buy is justified.

To identify the savings that the buyer has provided through quantity buying, apply the following steps:

1.   If no losses result from obsolescence or deterioration:
    a.   Subtract Percent Inventory Cost found in column 3 of Quantity Break Table from available yield (percentage price savings plus purchase-order savings).
    b.   Multiply remainder by total value of material procured to find savings in dollars.
2.   If losses were incurred due to deterioration or obsolescence:
    a.   Subtract deterioration and obsolescence losses from 1a. above.
    b.   Multiply remainder by total value of material procured to find savings in dollars.

As you have seen, identification of the purchase-order processing and price savings is separated into two steps and tables. There are alternate techniques that combine this cost-savings identification into one step. However, this particular format was chosen due to two distinct advantages that it provides. One is that the tables that result are much less formidable and, thus, more likely to be used in daily operation. Discussions with various purchasing managers and buyers indicate that the increased arithmetic associated with this method is preferable to the increased table complexity necessary in the alternate methods.

The second advantage stems from being able to determine cost sensitivity. The price savings is a "hard," guaranteed return. However, the purchase-order-processing savings for a particular critical decision is less justifiable. If you are in a position where cash is tight, workloads are down, or you are engaging in quantity buying only on a sporadic basis, it is important to identify and set priorities for quantity-buy opportunities on price advantage alone, rather than including purchase-order-processing savings. This procedure offers the option of identifying the significance of processing savings and/or ignoring them altogether.

Within the context of both of these procedures, there are methods available to enable you to remove the complexity normally associated with these decisions. By applying the table modification directions included in Appendix 6, you can also assure that escalation-hedge and quantity-break decisions reached through application of this procedure will be consistent with your company's financial objectives, and thus, will contribute to your company's financial well-being.

ORDER ELIMINATION

Order elimination (preventing an unnecessary order) could be included in a list of routine improvement activities. However, although order elimination can result in a cost improvement, this activity is very difficult to justify as a viable purchasing improvement function. The other techniques discussed have all had one thing in common. Purchasing participation was desirable due to the influence of vendor information on the decision being made and purchasing's unique vendor/organizational position.

With respect to order elimination, though, no market information is required. Purchasing should apply the same information that the requisitioner applies in identifying the requirement. This is an unnecessary duplication of effort. If there is assurance that the job was done correctly the first time, the expense required for purchasing participation would be unnecessary.

Consequently, it is recommended that this task be removed from purchasing by assuring that the requisitioner's search is thorough.

In order to assure a thorough requisitioner search, or in case such a search is not possible and purchasing must maintain the function, it would be desirable to have the following information readily available concerning inventoried materials for which quick turnover is questionable (surplus material):

1. General description
2. Material specification
3. Size and tolerance
4. Functional specification
5. Quantity on hand
6. Cost
7. Estimated scrap or resale value

This information will enable identification of whether the surplus material could serve as substitute for the requisitioned requirement. The use of this information should be self-explanatory with the exception, perhaps, of the functional specification and the estimated scrap or resale value. The functional specification is desirable in identifying instances in which an alternate stocked material (for instance, a steel valve) might substitute for the requisitioned material (cast iron valve) by performing the same or a higher-grade function. This specification should relate to the critical temperature, pressures, strength, flows, etc., of the commodity to facilitate selection (see the section on Redesign in Chapter 4, for instructions on determining the functional specifications).

Providing the estimated scrap or resale value along with the commodity listing would serve two purposes. One would be to prevent carrying the slow-moving item in inventory if the resale or scrap value closely approximated its original value. The other would be to prevent a functional upgrading such as that described above if the scrap value of the material was higher than the cost of the requisitioned material. In this case it would be less costly to scrap the stocked material and purchase requisitioned material than to use the stocked material instead. The scrap value can be identified through accounting records based on average disposal returns for similar commodities.

By providing arrangements of this list for suppliers' material sorted by general description for both material type and functional specification, the search for substitutes would be greatly facilitated.

To evaluate your savings contribution through elimination of an ordering requirement, the following formula may be applied:

Equation 4

$$\text{Elimination savings} = (P_1 Q_1 h) + (P.O.) + (P_2(Q_1) - S)$$

Where:
- P_1 = price of commodity in stock
- Q_1 = requisitioned quantity
- h = full accounting holding cost less deterioration (full cost used since space and labor apply)
- $P.O.$ = purchase order processing cost
- P_2 = price of requisitioned commodity
- S = scrap or sale value of $(P_1 Q_1)$

If the scrap or sale value is unavailable, replace $(P_2(Q_1) - S)$ with $(P_2 - P_1)$, the material savings obtained through using the stocked material rather than that requisitioned. Negative values should be ignored in this part of the equation with the assumption that the $(P_1 - S)$ is less than $(P_2 - P_1)$. An example application of this formula follows:

Assume that:
P_1 = Price of stocked substitute   = \$2000/unit
Q_1 = Quantity requisitioned   = 10 units
h = Hold cost   = 15%
$P.O.$ = Purchase order processing   = \$20
P_2 = Price of requisitioned commodity = \$1,800
S = Scrap/sales value of (P_1Q_1) = \$10,000

Elimination savings = (\$2000)(10)(.15) + 20 +
((\$1,800)(10)) − (\$10,000) = \$11,220

Once you have identified this savings, it becomes clear in this case that it is preferable to use the stocked surplus rather than engage in a purchase of alternate material even though the stocked material carried a higher purchase price. This outcome, however, is entirely dependent on the stocked material actually being surplus material.

If you are reviewing the benefit of using material in stock which is not considered surplus, this formula must be modified as follows:

Equation 5

Non-surplus elimination savings =

$$(P_1Q_1)\left(\frac{h}{52}\right)W) + (P.O.) + (P_2(Q_1) - (P_1Q_1))$$

Where: P_1 = price of commodity in stock
Q_1 = requisitioned quantity
h = holding cost
W = estimated number of weeks in stock
$P.O.$ = purchase-order processing cost
P_2 = price of requisitioned commodity

In the above example, if the estimated number of weeks (W) that this material is expected to remain in stock is 15, the elimination savings will be:

$$= (2,000(10)\left(\frac{.15}{52}\right)15) + 20 + ((18,000) - 20,000)$$
$$= -\$1,115.$$

In accordance with the above, you could not afford to use this stocked material in place of the requisitioned requirements.

The key to efficiency with each of these decisions is a thorough review and identification of the material stock compared to the requisitioned requirement. Again, this review should not take place in purchasing but instead the previous search and evaluation methods should be applied in conjunction with the requisitioning function.

NEW SOURCE DEVELOPMENT

New source development, however, is a distinct purchasing function. It can be approached on both a keying-improvement and routine-improvement level. This section covers routine new source development, which can be conducted efficiently in conjunction with normal daily activities.

New or previously unused vendors will be calling at regular intervals in an attempt to secure your business. By using the total-material-cost information discussed in Chapter 2, it is possible to pursue routine new source development productively in order to make these introductory calls more valuable.

The material-related cost information discussed in Chapter 2 will enable you to identify the highest-cost commodity within the vendor's capability. With this information, you can request a quotation on your highest potential commodity in his line. In this way the minimum unproductive time will be spent before finding if the vendor has the capability to serve you, since you will immediately be able to direct his activity towards your highest potential commodity.

To assist in this effort, it would also be beneficial to have at your disposal the following three tools: commodity, quantity, and price histories; functional specifications; and vendor facility lists. The commodity history will provide information concerning past quantities procured. This insight will be sufficient to provide the vendor with enough information on your commodity requirements to generate a quotation.

The functional specification (described in Chapter 4) will allow discussing the actual commodity requirements without getting embroiled in the intricacies of another vendor's unnecessary but offered features. For instance, if all you have to work with is a current vendor's style number, it would be rare that another vendor could precisely duplicate that style. However, it would even be rarer that once the unnecessary features are eliminated from the discussion that a competitive offering would not be available.

The facilities list of the current vendor will also lead to beneficial discussions by narrowing the new vendor's capability with respect to your commodities and facilitating comparisons with alternate manufacturing techniques.

If you do find an advantage (evaluated as in Chapter 2) in dealing with a new vendor, make sure that you have taken the necessary steps in qualifying this vendor before placing an order with him. For qualification directions, refer to Appendix 9.

SUMMARY

This chapter has discussed the evaluation methods and information requirements for the routine improvement techniques:

1. Combining and splitting of requisitions
2. Quantity-break buying
3. Price hedging
4. Elimination of orders
5. New source development

The daily situations that will present application possibilities for these techniques are summarized as follows:

1. *Combining requisitions.* Requisitions with similar required dates and material suitable for procurring from the same vendor should definitely be used to key combination activities. Savings will equate to purchase-order processing savings plus any price-transportation advantage available.

   Through the structure of your inquiry and application of the quantity-break technique it is possible to determine if requisitions with different required dates capable of being produced by the same vendor are also candidates for combination.

2. *Splitting requisitions.* Requisitions in which splitting items to more than one vendor would be a viable cost-savings attack can be determined by price histories or competitive quotations. Savings must be sufficient to offset increased purchase-order processing costs.

3. *Quantity-break.* Information concerning quantity-break advantages can and should be obtained through the structure of your inquiry or published price information. With the quantity-break cost advantage identified and through application of the methods described in this chapter, your decision to ignore or

take advantage of the quantity-break can be based on the total-cost effect.

4. *Price hedge*. Information concerning expected material-cost escalation should key this activity. Through application of the techniques identified with knowledge of expected inflation and material usage, it is possible to identify the optimum quantity of material to be ordered.

5. *Elimination*. With information concerning excess material in inventory, it is possible to engage in routine elimination activities. However, this activity duplicates the effort of the requisitioner and emphasis should be applied to the requisitioner performing a more complete function using the tools described in this chapter, rather than requiring purchasing to cross check his work.

6. *New source development*. A new vendor visit should key activity in requesting his quotation on your highest-cost commodity as identified by Chapter 2 data. In conjunction, a commodity history, functional specification, and a facility list should be available to lead to productive routine new source development.

All of these activities can be undertaken with a guaranteed yield for the time expended since the keying method is a part of your daily activities and the application techniques that have been reviewed are sufficiently structured to prevent a substantial time commitment in application.

=4

Keying-Improvement Techniques

The complete buyer is one who effectively applies the keying-improvement techniques: make-or-buy, contracting, redesign, and new source development; and who makes lowest-cost decisions in maintenance and routine improvement activities. This buyer provides the greatest possible contribution towards achieving your material-related-cost objectives.

However, few buyers today reach this level of excellence. Most fail to pursue keying-improvement applications, not because they are content to do an incomplete job, but because they cannot assure that the time required in this pursuit will be well spent. As a result, purchasing usually applies these techniques only when they are initiated by others, and a good deal of purchasing's improvement potential remains untapped.

To enable purchasing departments to realize this potential, a structure is required that will guide buyers to their highest-yield improvement projects and assure that they can reach a satisfactory conclusion in each improvement application. In other words, this structure must direct buyers to their highest potential commodities, select the optimum improvement technique for each of these commodities, and describe how to efficiently apply each technique.

You have already reviewed portions of such a structure in the first chapter of this book. This overview suggested that you can initiate this structuring process by identifying those commodities that contribute the greatest proportion or your company's total material-related cost, for it is these commodities that will provide the greatest potential for improvement. It was also proposed that once you have determined this "set" of high-potential commodities, you can select the optimum improvement technique to apply to each by analyzing the composition of its material-related cost contribution and by identifying the technique capable of influencing the greatest proportion of this cost. This analysis and identification process is summarized in Form 5, which can be used to compute your technique-cost relationships for each commodity.

FORM 5.   Keying Technique Application—Cost Relationship

Value-Analysis Technique	Influenced Material-Related Costs	Technique-Cost Grouping
Make or Buy	Price, manufacturing cost, lost profit due to restricted capacity.	
Contracting	Vendor profit, inventory cost, ordering cost, late delivery.	
Redesign	Price, insufficient-quality cost (claims cost, quality-related late delivery).	
New Source Development	Price highest individual cost and vendor is sole source or source-controlled.	

Commodity Description _____

Application of these steps will steer your improvement effort towards your highest potential commodity-technique considerations, and thus will identify the projects most significant to your company's profitability. As is evident, before initiating such an approach it is necessary to provide this total material-related cost information in a form convenient to the selection process. Obtaining this information will be the topic of the following discussion.

COST-COLLECTION AND APPLICATION PROCEDURE

A collection procedure for a portion of this cost information was already described in conjunction with the maintenance decisions. However, we must still discuss how to efficiently collect the required data concerning purchase-order processing cost, profit potential of products restricted by capacity, and manufacturing and inventory costs. The key to efficiency in this collection, as with preceding efforts, is to restrict your information gathering only to those commodities of the greatest cost significance rather than collecting information for all commodities before determining which are most important. As you will see, the following procedure applies this "greatest significance" approach in directing you to collect and compile the information as shown below:

1.   Information Collection
    a.   Request that manufacturing identify their 10 to 20 highest-

cost operations and provide the labor-cost contributions per commodity for each of these operations.[1]

  b. Request that each buyer identify the 10 commodities for which he spends the most per year, the amount per year, and price per piece.

  c. Request that inventory control identify their 10 to 20 largest inventory accounts with respect to commodity groupings and the associated annual holding cost per commodity.

  d. Review Chapter 2, Data Collection for results, identifying the 10 to 20 vendors contributing the largest delivery delay and insufficient-quality claims cost.

  e. Review results obtained from the clerical-cost collection form identified in Appendix 8 to determine the 10–20 highest clerical-processing-cost vendors and relate vendors identified to commodities handled.

  f. Request that marketing (sales) identify the 5 largest-profit potential products for which sales are restricted due to capacity limitations, and the resulting additional profit available if there were no capacity restrictions. Also request them to relate this profit to the highest-value material item contained in this product.

2. Compilation

  a. Sort above responses by commodity and table this information as in Form 6.

  b. In the event that there is not a perfect overlap of information (all costs are not completed for each listed commodity), refer back to information sources and complete information for commodities listed (with the exception of manufacturing cost).

  c. Total all costs referenced for commodities shown.

3. Identify techniques applicable to each commodity using applicable-cost method discussed above.

4. Initiate improvement applications by having each buyer select his 5 highest-cost commodities as determined above.

Through application of this procedure, not only will you obtain the necessary information to identify your highest-potential-improvement projects, but you have also given each of your interfacing departments an opportunity to play a part in this selection process. Consequently, you

---

[1]Request "Basic Make Costs" as displayed in the make-or-buy procedure that follows. Contributions per commodity may be specified in general terms if a mix of different types of commodities are manufactured, e.g., 1 hour labor per square foot of 3/16 plate or 1 hour labor per CWT of structural steel.

FORM 6.   Commodity Cost Composition

Description	Price	Dollar Value	Mfg. Cost Per Annum	Capacity Restricted Profit	Annual Inven. Cost	Delivery Delay	Annual Claims Cost	Annual Process. Cost
A-283 Steel Plate (size . . .)								
Fan, type . . .								
Etc.								

will have increased their motivation to provide assistance in reaching a successful conclusion to your improvement effort.

Once you have applied this procedure and have identified the commodity and keying-improvement technique that offers the greatest potential, you are still only halfway home. Application of each of these techniques can still be unrewarding and extremely time-consuming unless you proceed in an efficient manner. Consequently, let us review the approaches that will assure efficiency in each of these applications.

MAKE-OR-BUY

It is felt that purchasing-initiated make-or-buy efforts have received an unnecessarily poor reputation for improvement application. This situation appears to have occurred largely as a result of misunderstanding the intent of this function's value in both purchasing and manufacturing. A review of the causes of this misunderstanding will help to establish a make-or-buy perspective.

Make-or-buy decisions traditionally have been the prerogative of manufacturing, applied only in the case of shop-load fluctuation. If facilities were overloaded, a purchasing "buy" investigation was requested by manufacturing. If underloaded, items previously procured from outside vendors would be manufactured in-house as directed by the manufacturing group.

However, at times, as a result of vendor contact, purchasing would be expected to break this pattern and recommend a potential "buy" opportunity on their own. The result of this recommendation would be a conflict situation, in which purchasing is not only infringing on a traditional "manufacturing prerogative" (determining the point manufacture) but also threatening to decrease shop loads and increase shop inefficiency.

In this conflict atmosphere, manufacturing would be expected to attempt to overrule the purchasing recommendation through any means possible. If manufacturing was regularly successful, purchasing might react by vowing never again to waste their time initiating a make-or-buy proposal because "no matter what we find, we won't get work out of the shop."

Contrary to beliefs and experiences such as these, there is much to gain from purchasing-initiated make-or-buy efforts. However, this value is contributed not by winning or losing as the result of the make-or-buy verdict but by identifying the most efficient combination of design and point of manufacture. Fortunately, purchasing is in a unique organizational position to guide this identification effort, as a result of having numerous vendor-engineering and manufacturing groups at its disposal to review higher-cost components of the company's product and suggest alternate design and manufacturing directions. Further, regardless of the major point-of-manufacture decision that results from such a review, as long as information transmittal is properly structured and decision rules are agreed upon, are equitable, and produce a lowest-cost result, both the vendor and your organization will gain in manufacturing knowledge and profitability from this activity. With this in mind, let us delineate the requirements of an effective make-or-buy attack that will produce these results and provide the above "mutual benefit" framework.

Methodology

Unless it is absolutely impossible to make or to buy a commodity, the specific information requirements and decision criteria are so bound by the situation under investigation that no simple formula will provide an answer. However, by proceeding as instructed below, you will be able to reach a sound decision with the least possible effort, whether you are analyzing the point of manufacture of a whole plant's product or a commodity of no more significance than a single nut or bolt.

Structuring the Attack

As we have said, there are two roads leading to a make-or-buy analysis. One of these begins with someone outside of purchasing initiating the analysis as a result of vendor suggestions, capacity restrictions, or emergence of new components. In this case, a separate attack structure is unnecessary because the product to be analyzed and participants in the analysis have already been identified through circumstance.

The alternative to this process requires active pursuit of improvement. In the introduction to this chapter, we reviewed the foundation for this attack, how to identify those components or products with the highest make-or-buy potential, but we have yet to discuss the most beneficial attack organization.

In identifying these "prime" commodities, you will also have identified projects that will have a major profit, investment, and capacity influence on your company. Due to the importance of your decisions and the need for cooperation between disciplines, it is suggested that a committee-decision approach be adopted for these projects. This approach involves your top-ranking officers' endorsement of this program, and their designation of permanent committee participants from functions contributing to and affected by the make-or-buy analysis. As you will see in the following procedure, this membership should consist of purchasing, marketing or sales, production-inventory control, finance and accounting, manufacturing, and engineering.

Before convening the committee, this highest potential "set" of commodities should be narrowed to only those for which the "buy" option actually presents a viable alternative. This can be accomplished through a review of your vendor's capabilities. In this review you should eliminate those components for which you cannot locate a vendor capable of meeting your supply requirements. On completion of this step, the candidates for the make-or-buy analysis will have been identified and the two approaches, individual and committee, rejoin in the collection of the basic make-or-buy data.

Make-or-Buy Data Collection and Analysis

The following data and analysis are essential to a make-or-buy review regardless of the size of the component being investigated. Consequently, under either the individual or the improvement approach, Form 7 should be circulated with instructions to the recipients requesting them to review those items for which they have responsibility (referenced on the left side of the form) and to enter their answers at the right. Completion of this form will provide the basic make-or-buy costs and investments. This form also includes a procedure instructing the originator in how to determine the optimum decision direction. With the exception of Activity I, the originator's responsibility for obtaining information begins after this form has been returned from the referenced departments.

Through circulation and application of the instructions in this form, the buyer or committee originator can collect the basic make-or-buy information and identify the most beneficial decisions. Most of the information and approach applied in this procedure will be self-explanatory. However, it will help to discuss a notable omission, failure to include fixed overhead in the analysis, and the logic behind the treatment of qualitative considerations.

First, let us review the rationale for excluding fixed overhead. Unless the equipment, buildings, and personnel that constitute burden, general and administrative expense (G&A), and selling expense can be scrapped, sold, or released as a result of your decision, you will incur these costs regardless of the make-or-buy outcome. Further, since it is highly unlikely that these disposal options will be appropriate except in your largest make-or-buy projects, they are excluded from the preceding basic analysis. However, as you will see, this analysis has been included for application within the committee's activity.

The second point of elaboration includes the qualitative considera-

FORM 7. Make-or-Buy Review

Responsible Department	Activity	Result No.	Answer for Year			
			1	2	3	4
Originator	I. Contact Engineering to identify if a component is *proprietary*[1] in function. A. If it is, cancel the review B. If not, proceed with next step		Check one & reference person providing answer. ☐ Yes ☐ No Per			
Originator	II. Identify the *Term of Investment* to be used in this review by choosing the shortest of the following periods.		——— Term of Investment			
Engineering	A. Expected production run life of the component in question.		——— Years			
Finance	B. Desired Payback period.[2]		——— Years			
Purch./Manuf.	C. Period for which cost advantages appear permanent.		——— Years			
Prod. Cont.	III. Estimate *quantities* of component required per year for years 1, 2, 3, 4. IV. Identify make-and-buy costs A. *Make Cost* includes: 1. *Material Cost* for all material used in manufacture of component under review. Composed of:					

(Insert Component Description)_____ Date _____

[1] Proprietary may be defined as being of such unprotected (through patent, etc.) competitive value that release of a functional specification would threaten the competitive ability of the firm. Originator should determine if component is proprietary prior to distribution of this form.
[2] Payback period is defined as: Investment divided by annual net receipts available from the investment.

FORM 7. Make-or-Buy Review (continued)

Responsible Department	Activity	Result No.	Answer for Year			
			1	2	3	4
Purchasing	a. Purchase price[3]		+			
Purchasing	b. Terms-of-payment benefit[4]		–			
Purchasing	c. Price times "hidden-cost ratio"[5]		+			
	2. *Direct labor cost* per component composed of:					
Manufacturing	a. Set-up cost[6]		+			
Manufacturing	b. Unit labor-run charge		+			
Manufacturing	c. Subcontract cost per price (if applicable)		+			
	3. *Variable overhead* per price includes:					
Accounting	a. Indirect shop labor		+			
	b. Additional supervision		+			
	c. Compensation insurance		+			
	d. Machine maintenance		+			
	e. Overtime premium		+			
	f. Vacation pay		+			
	g. Social Security taxes		+			

(Insert Component Description)_____ Date _____

[3]Price should be identified on the basis of the economic price-break quantity as reviewed in Chapter 3 of this book.

[4]Compute based on net terms of payment valuation as reviewed in Chapter 2.

[5]Described in Chapter 2 of this book composed of freight, early-shipment cost, insufficient-quality cost, cost-improvement contribution and late-delivery cost.

[6]Set-up should be amortized on a per-component basis by dividing the number of pieces in the economic lot size (ELS) into the set-up cost. ELS is computed as follows:

$$ELS = \sqrt{\frac{2(C_s)(S_m)}{h_c}}$$

Where: C_s = Set-up Cost
S_m = Annual number of components used in dollars
h_c = Annual holding cost per component in dollars

FORM 7. Make-or-Buy Review (continued)

Responsible Department	Activity	Result No.	Answer for Year 1	2	3	4
Manufacturing	4. Cost of *expense tooling* amortized per component for the life of the investment.		+			
	5. Total above costs to determine basic make cost.	MC				
Originator	6. Multiply each (MC) answer by applicable annual quantities to determine annual make cost.	AMC				
	7. Identify total make costs for term of the investment.	TMC =	= Total of all (AMC) answers			
Purchasing	B. Compute *basic buy cost*					
	1. Add:					
	a. Purchase price [7]		+			
	b. Terms of payment benefit [8]		−			
	c. Price times "hidden cost ratio" [9]		+			
	d. Cost of expense tooling amortized per component for term of investment.	BC	+			
	2. Multiply each (BC) answer by applicable annual quantities to determine annual buy cost.	ABC				

(Insert Component Description) _____ Date _____

[7] Price should be identified on the basis of the economic price-break quantity as reviewed in Chapter 3 of this book.

[8] Compute based on net terms of payment valuation as reviewed in Chapter 2.

[9] Described in Chapter 2 of this book composed of freight, early shipment cost, insufficient-quality cost, cost-improvement contribution and late-delivery cost.

FORM 7. Make-or-Buy Review (continued)

Responsible Department	Activity	Result No.	Answer for Year			
			1	2	3	4
Prod. Control (If buy is reviewed)	3. Identify total buy costs for term of investment.	TBC =	= Total of all (ABC) answers			
	C. Will existing vendor or company *inventory* for which we are responsible be obsolete as a result of this change?		Check One: ☐ Yes ☐ No			
	1. If no, omit analysis below.					
Purchasing (If make is reviewed)	2. If yes,					
	a. Identify value of affected inventory.					
	b. Identify return for scrapping.					
	c. Identify number of components that could be manufactured from this inventory.					
Originator	d. Identify scrap cost per component.	ISC	$= \dfrac{(\text{Inventory Value}) - (\text{Scrap Return})}{\text{Quantity}}$			
	V. Identify magnitude of investments required.					
	A. *"Make" investment*					
Prod. Control	1. Average work-in-progress inventory.					
Prod. Control	2. Average raw-material inventory.					
Prod. Control	3. Average finished-goods inventory.					
Manufacturing	4. Capital-equipment outlay required.					
Originator	5. Total of above.	MI				

(Insert Component Description) _____ Date _____

FORM 7. Make-or-Buy Review (continued)

Responsible Department	Activity	Result No.	Answer for Year			
			1	2	3	4
	B. "Buy" Investment					
	1. Average finished-goods inventories (same as 3 above).					
Purchasing	2. Necessary capital outlay					
Originator	3. Total of above	BI				
Manufacturing	C. Is there an *alternate component(s)*[10] that can utilize existing equipment vacated by this decision? Describe this component here.	AI	Check One: ☐ Yes ☐ No Description			
	1. If there is, what investment would be required if the above equipment was not available?					
	2. What would this alternate component cost if made using this vacated equipment (attach copy of basic Make-or-Buy cost derived as directed by step IV)?					
	3. What would it cost if investment was made (attach documentation as instructed above)?					
Originator[11]	4. What quantities of this component will be required per year?					
	5. Subtract (2 minus 3) and show savings per year (quantity times this remainder).	AC				
	6. Identify *total of AC answers.*	TAC				

(Insert Component Description) _____ Date _____

[10] Note: Review only if equipment is currently at 70 percent or greater capacity.
[11] Contact Production Control on return of form to identify.

FORM 7. Make-or-Buy Review (continued)

Responsible Department	Activity	Result No.	Answer for Year			
			1	2	3	4
	VI. Determine if *qualitative factors*, below, are of enough concern to restrict decision direction (Indicate yes[12] or no to the right of each concern).					
Engineering	A: Quality		☐ Yes ☐ No			
Manuf./Person.	B. Employee morale		☐ Yes ☐ No			
Prod. Control	C. Control		☐ Yes ☐ No			
Prod. Control	D. Assurance of supply		☐ Yes ☐ No			
	E. Union contractual obligations		☐ Yes ☐ No			
Originator	VII. Identify *decision direction* by determining if A or B below is applicable and following the steps outlined.					
	A. *If there is no investment* identified in results MI, BI or AI, proceed with steps 1 or 2 below.					
	1. If result of "AC" is less than zero:					
	a. Identify if change in point of manufacture saves more than 15%[14]					
	b. If it does, recommend change and use of existing equipment for alternate component manufacture.					

Savings Computation

For: Make Investigation $= \dfrac{TBC - (TMC - |TAC|^{[13]}) \times 100}{TBC} =$ ____

Buy Investigation $= \dfrac{TMC - (BC - |TAC|) \times 100}{TMC} =$ ____

Note: Use only if alternate component cost is analyzed.

(Insert Component Description) _____   Date _____

[12] If yes, include explanatory documentation.
[13] |TAC| instructs you to use the result of (TAC) but to ignore the sign (+ or −) in your computations.
[14] Risk factor for change in point of manufacture.

FORM 7. Make-or-Buy Review (continued)

Responsible Department	Activity	Result No.	Answer for Year 1	2	3	4

Note: Use if no alternate component cost.	2. If the result of "AC" is equal to or greater than zero:
	  a. Identify if change in point of manufacture saves more than 15%[15]
	  b. If it does, recommend change but do not use vacated equipment for manufacture of alternate component.
		Savings Computation
		
		For: Make Investigation $= \dfrac{TBC - TMC}{TBC} \times 100 =$
		
		For: Buy Investigation $= \dfrac{TMC - TBC}{TMC} \times 100 =$				

Originator	B. If there is an *investment required* proceed as follows: 1. Identify if ROI is greater than 30%[16]. If it is, recommend change.	*ROI Computation* For: Make Investigation $= \dfrac{TBC - TMC}{1/2\ (MI)} \times 100 =$ Buy Investigation $= \dfrac{TMC - TBC}{1/2\ (BI)} \times 100 =$				
(Omit if no alternate component identified)	2. If Alternate ROI is greater than ROI, also recommend that alternate component use existing equipment.	*Alternate ROI* For: Make Investigation $= \dfrac{TBC - (TMC + TAC)}{1/2\ (MI - AI)} \times 100 =$ For: Buy Investigation $= \dfrac{(TMC - (TBC + TAC)}{1/2\ (BI - AI)} \times 100 =$				

(Insert Component Description) _____ _____ Date _____

[15] Risk factor plus necessary "No Risk" return necessary to justify investment.
[16] Risk factor plus necessary return necessary to justify investment.

FORM 7. Make-or-Buy Review (continued)

Responsible Department	Activity	Result No.	Answer for Year			
			1	2	3	4
Originator	C. Use of existing inventory		Check Applicable Box			
	1. Is the difference between unit make-and-buy costs (MC and BC) greater than (ISC)?		☐ Yes ☐ No			
	2. If it is not, withhold implementation until inventories are utilized.					
	3. If it is, implement decision immediately and scrap or sell existing inventories.					
	D. If a change in manufacture is recommended above but the qualitative factors are of concern, split the component volume between the make-or-buy alternatives. In this case, neither make nor buy should receive less than 25% of the expected volume.					
	E. If investment is over $5,000, make-or-buy cost is greater than $100,000[17] per annum, or if you cannot reach a satisfactory point of manufacture agreement through following the directions in this procedure, provide analysis to make-or-buy committee for final recommendation.		Check application situation: Investment over $5,000 ___ Volume over $100,000 ___ No Agreement ___			
	F. Distribute final recommendation to all parties that have been involved in this procedure.					

(Insert Component Description) _____ Date _____

[17] These are arbitrary cutoffs. Refer to your financial department for establishment of suitable limits for your company.

tions of quality, employee morale, control, assurance of supply, and union contractual commitments.

These factors have served as a major stumbling block to many make-or-buy procedures because they are difficult to evaluate except in an intuitive manner, without having some experience with the alternative (either make or buy). However, none of these qualitative considerations should serve as permanent roadblocks to change; first further experience is necessary with respect to the actual cost of these concerns.

Instead of arbitrarily reversing the decision, it will be beneficial from many standpoints to split the production between both the make and the buy alternative in proportions comparable to the seriousness of the concern to gain experience that would allow disregarding or quantifying this consideration. For instance, if the quality of an untried vendor was of concern but an investment advantage was identified for the buy alternative, it would be worthwhile to test that vendor on a participative basis with a portion of the business. This testing and trial process will not only enable you to assure the appropriateness of your decision through obtaining actual experience with this potential cost, but will also build credibility in the sincerity of your make-or-buy effort — since a reward would be forthcoming for a quantifiable advantage, demonstrating that the decision was made on a competitive basis and that you will provide the vendor or shop the opportunity to remove the qualitative objection through actual performance.

To this point, we have reviewed make-or-buy initiation from the reactive and improvement paths, the accompanying information requirements, and collection methods. One important aspect has been omitted, however, concerning a critical purchasing obligation in this data-collection effort. This concerns the form in which vendor data should be requested in order to benefit most from make-or-buy projects.

Process-Data Gathering

In accordance with the more traditional make-or-buy approach, purchasing's primary input has been restricted to obtaining the buy price and the cost of purchased materials used in the make alternative. However, purchasing has a much greater responsibility than just identifying what will be paid to vendors. To illustrate this responsibility, let us assume that a make-or-buy review has been completed and a "buy" recommendation results. The analysis cannot be allowed to stop at this point; there is still much to be learned from this result.

For instance, how is the vendor able to supply the same part covering fixed overhead, G&A, and profit for less than your shop's variable costs? Is there a process or technique omitted that should have been included or that was unnecessary in the internal manufacturing process? If for no other reason than to facilitate a proper decision, it is necessary to review the production method and process suggested by the vendor; but it is this information and review that provides the basis for not only a good decision, but a cross-fertilization of manufacturing techniques as well.

To provide these data and accumulate buy costs, it is necessary for the inquiry to make clear to the vendors what information must be available for evaluation of their proposal and the ground rules under which the make-or-buy decision will be reached, assuring them that information will not be used indiscreetly. At the same time, the inquiry must provide the flexibility to let the vendor do his own thinking as to the most economical method of meeting your requirements.

These objectives may be accomplished by structuring the inquiry as follows:

1. Include only a broad functional description of the product as described in the Redesign portion of this chapter.
2. Request a vendor process description detailing equipment used, production flow, materials selected, and estimated man-hours by stage of production.
3. Assure that your vendor will receive like information concerning your manufacturing process.
4. Include the preceding make-or-buy decision description and rules.

By using this inquiry structure and with the proper reward for vendors facilitating improvements (i.e., a share of all of the business), the vendor will be encouraged to cooperate in facilitating your make-or-buy effort. Once this information is returned in the form of a quoted offering, and the similar manufacturing questionnaire information is returned from your own organization, there will be sufficient input to engage in a productive make-or-buy manufacturing review analysis and to learn how to improve overall operations.

Committee Participation

Through application of these procedures, you will be able to successfully conclude 80 to 90 percent of the make-or-buy reviews at an operating level. However, for:

1. The highest-priority make-or-buy projects,
2. Those "lower-level" projects requiring over a $5,000 investment or requiring a volume shift over $100,000, and

3. Those "lower-level" projects for which an acceptable outcome could not be reached through the preceding directions,

the make-or-buy committee must be convened to establish a course of action. In order to make these meetings most profitable, it is strongly recommended that an agenda listing open projects and related analysis sheets should be mailed prior to each session. Further, the agenda should request each member to review the probability of these new projects:

1. Changing G & A and selling expense requirements.
2. Enabling scrapping or sale of existing buildings or equipment.
3. Being distorted by the omission of learning-curve analysis.

Finally, the agenda should also request that your finance department apply a comprehensive financial analysis to the investments and returns for each project.

When the committee convenes, its charge is to jointly review and criticize these results in order to determine the most profitable decision direction. Before the meeting's conclusion, each project should be slotted into one of the following action categories:

1. Shelve projects with an unsatisfactory yield.
2. Determine and assign responsibility for initiating those projects with demonstrated quantitative potential.
   a. Identify related or spin-off projects.
   b. Establish suitable splits of business between make-and-buy alternatives if necessary.
3. Identify those projects that require further analysis, due to G & A, scrap or sale options, or learning-curve consideration[1] and request that the following form be completed prior to the next meeting to incorporate these considerations.

The committee should then reconvene monthly to follow the progress and actual results of these projects, determine outcomes of new projects that could not be resolved at operating levels, and initiate action on any other opportunities identified. Now, let us leave the actual "change of manufacture" decision and discuss how a buyer should determine what an equitable contract price would be for a buy recommendation.

[1]Refer to the following "Target Pricing" discussion for a review of learning-curve influences.

FORM 8. Fixed Cost-Learning-Curve Adjustment: Make-or-Buy Review

Responsible Department	Activity	Result No.	Answer for Year			
			1	2	3	4
Finance	I. Value *G&A Selling Expense Savings:*					
	A. If "buy" would result in decrease,					
	1. Identify value of decrease per year.					
	2. Compute decrease value per component by dividing by component annual quantity.					
	3. Add this value to make cost and recompute returns.					
	B. If "make" would result in increase,					
	1. Identify value of increase per year.					
	2. Compute increase value per component by dividing by component annual quantity.					
	3. Add this result to make cost and recompute returns.					
	II. Value return available from sale or scrap of existing buildings and machinery					
Manufacturing	A. What other components would have to be shifted to alternate facilities if this equipment was sold or scrapped, and what is the annual cost (volume) of each (compute basic make-or-buy costs)	Component #		Description/Annual Cost		
		1				
		2				
		3				
		4				
	1. What would be the annual cost savings (–) or penalty (+) incurred thru producing these components using alternate facilities (circle + or –)?	1	±	±	±	
		2	±	±	±	
		3	±	±	±	
		4	±	±	±	
		Total				

_____ Date _____

(Insert Component Description)

FORM 8. Fixed Cost–Learning-Curve Adjustment: Make-or-Buy Review (continued)

Responsible Department	Activity	Result No.	Answer for Year			
			1	2	3	4
Finance	2. Divide this savings/penalty by annual quantities of make-or-buy component and enter results.	S				
	3. Subtract (S) from buy cost if savings	SMC				
	4. Add (S) to buy cost if penalty.	SBC				
Finance	B. Adjust buy investment for scrap or sale credit.					
	1. Determine book value of facilities.					
	2. Annual depreciation value of these facilities.					
Purchasing	3. Resale or scrap value of these facilities.					
Finance	4. If book value is greater than resale or scrap value, determine buy investment credit as shown to the right.	Inv. Credit	$= \text{Resale} + \left[\left(\begin{smallmatrix} \text{Book} - \text{Resale} \\ \text{Value} \quad \text{Value} \end{smallmatrix} \right) \left(\begin{smallmatrix} 1 - \text{Tax} \\ \text{Rate} \end{smallmatrix} \right) \right]$			
	5. If book value is less than the resale or scrap value, determine buy-investment credit as shown to the right.	Inv. Credit	$= \text{Book} + \left[\left(\begin{smallmatrix} \text{Resale} - \text{Book} \\ \text{Value} \quad \text{Value} \end{smallmatrix} \right) \left(\begin{smallmatrix} 1 - \text{Tax} \\ \text{Rate} \end{smallmatrix} \right) \right]$			
Manufacturing	III. Adjust costs for learning curve influence[1]					
	A. Graph learning curve and identify position of make cost estimate.					
Finance	B. Recompute results using cost at point where curve levels.					

(Insert Component Description) _____ Date _____

[1] Refer to target pricing discussion of this chapter for learning curve discussion.

88

Target Pricing

Assuming that a buy decision has resulted from application of this procedure, it is then necessary to identify the proper price in order to provide factual targets for negotiation. Important tools in providing target information are manufacturing estimates of cost and learning-curve influence, and functional semi-log plots. Obviously, your minimum target position will be the vendor's quoted price and terms of payment. Whether there will or should be subsequent negotiations will depend on the credibility of the offering with respect to the analysis below.

With the aid of the vendor's processsing and material description, it should be possible for a manufacturing estimator to provide an alternate man-hour-material cost estimate to provide one of the target inputs. Manufacturing experience will also give an indication of the cost improvement·that should be expected through experience with the component. As one becomes more familiar with the requirements of producing a part, a cost reduction should result from more fluid processing and efficient materials utilization. This process has been empirically expressed in the form of the learning curve in Figure 6. Based on the

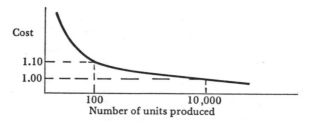

FIGURE 6.   Typical Learning Curve

learning-curve experience in your manufacturing department and their cost estimate for a high number of repetitions, it will be possible to place the vendor's quotation on this curve and negotiate the learning phase contribution. In the above example, if the vendor's quoted price is $1.10 and the cost estimate where the curve began to level was $1.00, the expected learning-curve reduction would be (1.10 − 1.00) or 10 cents.

Before you try applying a learning curve to your vendor, however, the following questions must be answered.[1]

1. Is the item in question one that represents a new manufacturing procedure for him? Whether or not this is the first order you

[1]"Learning Curve: A Negotiation Tool", *Purchasing* 73 (Sept. 19, 1972): 102–104.

have placed with him is irrelevant. If this is a standard item for his plant, or one that he has been producing for some time, then the learning curve would have flattened out long ago. In this case, the cost difference would involve estimating discrepancies and the learning-curve approach should be ignored.

2. How well did the vendor plan the operation before going into initial production? If your supplier sets up too quickly, without sufficient forethought and research, chances for errors are high. Since improvement will be erratic and probably unpatterned, no formula can be successfully applied. Consequently, the learning-curve extrapolation must be ignored.

In addition to the above inputs, by plotting cost against functional performance criteria it is possible to support the above estimate and/or provide supplemental information. For a pump, the plot might be reviewed as in Figure 7. If your price was in accordance with Level X in Figure 7, and if you did request a functional offering from your vendor, it can be inferred that the cost difference between points X and Y is excessive, and that further review to identify why this differential exists would be beneficial.

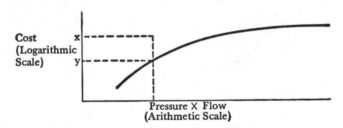

FIGURE 7. Cost/Function Relationship

With this information you have identified and supported, through analysis, a maximum (the manufacturing-functional cost result) and minimum target (the vendor's original offering). Your negotiations should progress using the data discussed for the maximum target to a mutual settlement in the intermediate area.

However, before concluding negotiation, it is also necessary to assure that your saving advantage will be available long enough to enable you to return your investment. Obtaining this protection in most cases will require that you include a maximum price-escalation clause in your contract in accordance with your vendor's expected cost increases, to prevent excessive escalation once you are committed to this course of action.

CONTRACTING

Purchasing contracting efforts, unlike make-or-buy and respecification, have usually been considered by other departments to be an unquestioned purchasing prerogative and have enjoyed a reputation for being an effective means of reducing costs. Many purchasing contracts, however, do not deserve this favorable reputation when one considers the long-term costs resulting from these agreements.

In the most typical contracting application, volume or leverage contracting, purchasing will ask vendors to bid on the total annual dollar volume of a certain commodity or commodity grouping (e.g., drills, carbon steel, etc.). Purchasing will offer no increased discipline in maximum or minimum release quantities and no guarantee that the full volume will be procured in the year offered (typical conditions associated with blanket orders or letters of intent). As a result of these provisions, the vendor is offered very little, if any, increased production efficiency. Yet the buyer expects a significant price reduction for these commitments. As stated by E. L. Anderson (*Purchasing World*, March 1973):[1]

> Purchasing people are having trouble writing contracts today [referring to the tight markets existing in 1973] for a simple reason. The past two or three years have seen vendors beaten to death with blanket orders. . . . I haven't seen the supplier yet who likes blankets. They'll go along to meet competition, or to stay in the marketplace, but not because they think blankets are good business.

In this atmosphere any savings obtained will be temporary. The vendor will bend when forced but will recoup losses when the market tightens.

In order to contract effectively to produce long-term gains from your efforts, it is necessary to assure that mutual benefit is obtained and that for certain types of commodities the contracting effort attacks more than just the vendor's profit margin (systems contracting). Consequently, the remainder of this discussion deals with the requirements of effective contracting by describing when and how to apply specific contracting techniques. In this discussion contracting is divided into two subcategories: volume and system contracting. Volume contracting, since it is the least complicated and most generally applied, will be discussed first.

[1]Brook Elliot, "The Case Against Blanket Orders," *Purchasing World* 17 (March 1973): 18.

Volume Contracting

The type of contracting referred to above (no-release discipline) has been titled "volume" contracting for purposes of this discussion. There are arguments both pro and con concerning the value of this activity. There is, however, one point of agreement in both arguments stated thus: Volume contracting is opportunistic in that a vendor will be interested in maintaining or receiving a greater share of your business at a reduced profit margin only if he does not have sufficient "profitable" business available.

The point of contention with respect to the value of volume contracting revolves around the total material-cost benefits actually realized as a result of a volume-contracting application.

The argument in favor of volume contracting states that this activity is beneficial in the long term; that the price concessions reflect the vendor's savings obtained through being able to assure that he will cover his fixed costs during low production periods. Consequently, there will be no adverse effects from such contracting. Gains will be temporary but should not be disregarded since there will be mutual benefit and therefore no negative offsets.

However, the alternate argument suggests that forcing a vendor to cut his price when he has the greatest need for profitable operations leads to shortcuts resulting in poor delivery and quality. When the market firms and supply is tight, your gains will turn into losses in further delivery delays and quality defects. In other words, you will not be a "favored" customer and will be forced to pay the price connected with your status as a result of opportunistic contracting.

Each argument is valid under certain conditions. Obtaining the answers to the following situational considerations will enable you to determine appropriate applications and engage in more effective volume contracting:

1. Is demand in the industry more than 30 percent below capacity?
2. Does the commodity grouping have an identifiable list price?
3. Are there many suppliers capable of supplying your requirements?
4. Is discounting an industry practice?

If the answers to these questions are yes, you can feel secure that volume contracting should be pursued and will result in temporary gains without significant long-term losses; but rather than accepting this on faith, let us review the significance of each of these questions.

The 70 percent demand-capacity ratio provides a fairly common rule of thumb concerning production efficiency. Most industries can operate efficiently at 80 percent and above but concern, with respect to overhead utilization, builds below 70 percent. Consequently, at this point companies begin looking for ways to assure utilization of their excess capacity. These will often include volume discounting to obtain a greater share of the market or maintain their existing share. Thus, through this review, you can identify the "market readiness" to contract based on capacity utilization in the industry.

However, even if the market is "ready," if the commodity does not have an identified list price, the favored approach to contracting would be the system-contracting approach that will be discussed in the next chapter. Since you must, in order to "tie down a price" for this type of commodity, specifically identify the types of commodities and quantities that will be procured, and because providing this identification can be fairly expensive, the system-contracting alternative offers a greater possibility of return because it attacks more than just vendor profit. However, if the commodity does carry a list price, you can usually volume-contract effectively by simply offering an annual volume in return for a "discount off list" which will identify the price applicable to each purchase.

The next consideration, whether many suppliers are capable of producing the commodity in question, must be reviewed in order to determine if you can expect quality and delivery to fall off as a response to the vendor's profit cut resulting from volume contracting. It is a safe bet that through competitive pressure you can demand performance with many suppliers available even though your contract produces opportunistic price-profit gains. With few suppliers, it is more likely that you will pay the penalty of poor quality and delivery when discounts are demanded.

Finally, if discounting is an industry practice, in effect you are forced to request the discount when the opportunity arises, since your competition will have the same opportunity. This identification requires market and competitive intelligence on your part.

Volume-Contracting Information Requirements

Information requirements to enable you to engage in effective volume contracting for the types of commodities described by the above considerations are fairly simple to obtain. All that is required to issue an inquiry is a forecasted volume of the commodity-grouping usage.

Reasonably accurate forecasts for volume contracting are not difficult to provide. Since, in volume contracting, you are usually interested in committing a group of commodities rather than one specific commodity, your demands for that commodity grouping will have a close relationship to the workload scheduled in the shops that use it.

Consequently, a forecast can be obtained simply by calculating past usage by applicable expected shop loads as follows:

$$\text{Estimated 1974 Usage} = \frac{\text{Shop man-hours 1974}}{\text{Shop man-hours 1973}} \times \text{1973 usage}$$

This method assumes a direct relationship between man-hours and historical usage. In order to verify this assumption and to insure accuracy you may want to confirm or modify the relationship using figures from more than just the last year.

The value of the integrity of your commitment cannot be stressed highly enough, with respect to assuring gain from your efforts. If you have promised the vendor $100,000 of business for this concession and only provide $40,000, you will have an extremely difficult task in attempting to reissue your contract or prevent vendor attempts at recouping lost profit. In most cases, a 10 percent negative deviation will be acceptable; a 20 percent deviation will jeopardize future activities. Consequently, it is recommended that your commitment estimate be conservative and based on projected information as outlined above rather than on history alone.

Offer Valuation

There are many techniques available to aid you in valuing a vendor's offer. The most commonly used is competitive bidding. Other aids such as price indexes from the Bureau of Labor Statistics and indexes from general purchasing or commodity publications, though less frequently used, are equally valuable. These indexes may be used to identify the relationship of your contract's price change to market changes.

By comparing past indexes to current ones, it is possible to identify market price changes. Relating these market changes to your changes from previous prices to contractually offered prices provides insight with respect to the competitiveness of the offer relative to market movements. I have observed situations in which buyers were offered no significant advantage for committing their total volume through an annual contract, and yet they contracted anyway, not realizing that the advantage identified was not the result of the contract but simply of market movements. Index analysis can prevent this lack of "market feel" that results in a disadvantageous contract.

Even in analyzing competitive bids, a few words of caution beyond those direct-costing considerations in the vendor-selection portion of Chapter 2 should be heeded. Most volume-contract offers from vendors will be in the form of a discount off list price. However, if list prices vary between vendors, you cannot tell without further analysis whether a 15 percent discount from one vendor is better than a 10 percent discount from another. To assure that you can identify the price differential available in this case, you should review sample net costs and estimate what percentage of your volume falls in each sample category. For instance, if you were presented with the list prices and discount quotations in Figure 8, by computing the effective cost it becomes clear that Vendor A offers no advantage at all and instead, Vendor B is 11 percent lower than Vendor A $\left(\left(1 - \dfrac{2.131}{2.385}\right) = 11\%\right)$.

Further, many buyers consider that the price advantage available from discounts can be calculated by simply subtracting one from the other. In other words, if Vendors A and B have identical lists and offer 40 percent and 45 percent discounts, respectively, many buyers would assume that Vendor B provided a 5 percent price advantage (45 percent − 40 percent). However, you must be careful when working with these percentages. For every dollar of list value for Vendor A you pay 60¢, whereas for Vendor B you only pay 55¢. Consequently, the percentage advantage for Vendor B is not 5 percent but 8 percent $\left(1 - \dfrac{.55}{.60}\right)$. In order to guard against miscalculations of savings, you are advised to compute the advantage available using the following formula as was done in the above example:

Equation 6

% Price Advantage Vendor B compared to Vendor A $=$

$$\left(1 - \frac{(100 - \% \text{ Discount Vendor B})}{(100 - \% \text{ Discount Vendor A})}\right) \times 100$$

Finally as with the make-or-buy decision, if the most favorable offer you have received involves a change of vendor from your previous standard, be sure that your price is protected either through firm pricing or maximum escalation for a period long enough so that you can economically reintroduce competition at the conclusion of your contract. Methods to forecast escalation in order to determine equitable escalation terms are portrayed in Appendix 11. Now, let us review the requirements and benefits of systems contracting.

FIGURE 8. Price-Discount Valuation

Tool Type	Vendor A					Vendor B				
	1 *List Price*	2 *Discount*	3 *Net Price*	4 *% Volume*	5 *Effective Cost – Col. 4 × 3*	1 *List Price*	2 *Discount*	3 *Net Price*	4 *% Volume*	5 *Effective Cost – Col. 4 × 3*
A	1.00	0.15	0.85	0.10	0.085	0.90	0.10	0.81	0.10	0.081
B	2.00	0.15	1.70	0.60	1.020	1.60	0.10	1.44	0.60	0.860
C	5.00	0.15	4.25	0.30	1.280	4.40	0.10	3.96	0.30	1.190
					Total 2.385					Total 2.131

SYSTEMS CONTRACTING

Systems contracting has application to a much broader group of commodities than does volume contracting, since it attacks material-related cost areas other than just vendor profit and thus provides continuing rather than opportunistic benefits for both buyer and seller. The systems-contracting technique that will be described requires a modification of your ordering method through your contract in order to provide the lowest-total vendor-buyer material-related cost.

The basic ordering modification in this type of contracting is a term commitment, usually a year or greater, for a firm quantity with prespecified release patterns. This procurement method is different from quantity–price-break buying in that you do not accept the full quantity at one time. Instead, you offer the vendor the flexibility to schedule, process, and produce in the most economical batches possible within your release pattern and firm quantity commitment, while asking him if it is economical to perform a portion of the inventory function. This flexibility and your firm commitment offer will allow identification of the lowest-cost, vendor-buyer ordering alternative.

As stated in the introduction to this section, this type of contracting has the greatest potential for influencing the material-related costs of vendor profit, ordering cost, and inventory. In order to allow this potential to be realized, however, a detailed material-requirement forecast may at times be necessary. General approaches to requirements forecasting are reviewed in Appendix 10. The discussion below deals with the information requirements of a contracting, material-requirements forecast. These requirements virtually restrict "systems" contracting to stock material or those purchase-for-contract materials for which such a forecast is feasible.

As mentioned above, in order to enable analysis of total processing, production, inventory, and transportation costs, it is necessary to identify the ordering alternative that minimizes these costs for the vendor and buyer. The soundest selection method for this optimum alternative requires an accurate forecast that displays a long-term estimate (one year or more) of the total quantity required and also provides information on how this commodity is likely to be used during the forecast period (i.e., maximum-minimum manufacturing demand per month).

If providing accurate forecasts for varying lengths of forecast periods did not carry increasing costs, it would be relatively unimportant to attempt to identify the optimum period of forecast prior to its generation. However, in general, costs of obtaining accurate commodity forecasts could be displayed as in Figure 9.

In a job-shop business where no two production units are exactly the

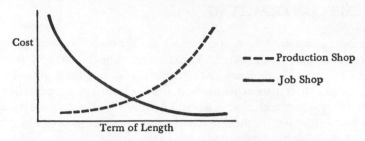

FIGURE 9. Forecasting Cost

same, short-term forecast accuracy is much more costly than accurate long-term annual forecasts. Over the longer term commodity-usage variations between units will average out. In the short term, however, the magnitudes of these variations must be identified and included in the forecast. Thus, short-term accuracy requires a much more complex review and a greatly increased forecast cost compared to long-term accuracy.

In a production shop, the opposite relationship will usually hold true. Standardized products will each use the same type and magnitude of materials. Due to this standardization, however, leadtimes are usually shorter and the exact production runs less capable of being forecasted. Consequently, in the short run, the sales-production forecast is relatively precise and material usage is known. In the long run, uncertainties as to the specific product lines in the sales forecast will add complexity to accurate forecasting and increase costs for long-term forecast accuracy.

Before providing the more expensive forecast in either case, it will be valuable to know if refining the forecast further will be of sufficient benefit to justify the cost. The method suggested for accomplishing this will be labeled "alternative bidding." This technique uses the basic (least expensive) forecast to generate combination, commitment, and release alternatives for inquiry purposes.

Alternative Bidding

The objective in the contracting activity is to identify the contracting alternative that is the least costly for both you and the vendor. To do this, it is necessary to structure the commitment and forecast alternatives in a manner that will enable you to identify the vendor's least-cost alternative which, in conjunction with your own information, will enable you to identify this lowest-total-cost option.

In order to obtain this information it is suggested that your inquiry be structured as follows:

1. *Intent and firm-commitment clause*
   a. Identify the estimated annual quantity that you are offering by commodity.
   b. Describe the intent of your inquiry.

      (E.g., This inquiry has been issued in the form below in order to allow you through your quotation of alternatives to identify the most economical form in which this contract should be issued. Flexibility in release disciplines has been provided through these alternatives to allow you via your quotation to identify those alternatives that minimize your handling, production, inventory, and transportation expense.)

2. *Release-commitment alternatives*
   Request that the 15 release-commitment options tabled in Form 9 be quoted. Further, explain that:
   a. *Release Quantity*
      Identifies maximum number of shipments and maximum movement out of vendor inventory. Number represents the fraction to be used in converting annual usage to release value or quantity. The initial release will be required within one leadtime period after contracting. Vendor must stock to provide next shipment one month after release.
   b. *Firm-Quantity Commitments*
      Identifies flexibility offered to vendor in terms of production-inventory options. (E.g., If release quantity is 1/12 and firm-quantity commitments is 1 year (option 4) the vendor has the greatest amount of flexibility. He may produce or procure only in monthly quantities incurring no inventory expense, or any of the arrangements in between.)
   c. *Option Price Per Piece*
      Request vendor to quote net price and transportation cost per piece applicable to each option.

3. *Price Protection*
   Request firm price or maximum escalation covering a period long enough to insure that you are able to reintroduce competition without losing a substantial proportion of your initial savings. Methods for forecasting inflation in order to determine an equitable protection clause are portrayed in Appendix 11. As in the other techniques, you would not want to stop at one-year protection if you know that you would not be able to reopen competitive bidding due to change-over costs until two years had passed, because you would be needlessly creating a sole-source vendor after the expiration of the first year.

FORM 9. Alternative Bidding Form

Option Number	Release Quantity[a] (fraction annual estimate)	Firm Quantity[b] Commitments (fraction annual estimate)	Option Cost[c] Per Piece	
			Price	Transportation
1				
2	1/12	2/12		
3		3/12		
4		6/12		
		1		
5	2/12	4/12		
6		6/12		
7		1		
8		3/12		
9	3/12	6/12		
10		1		
11	4/12	4/12		
12		8/12		
13		1		
14	6/12	6/12		
15		1		

[a,b,c]See accompanying outline.

Selection of Alternatives

Your choice of these alternatives for contracting will depend on the effect of each on total costs. The costs under consideration are those of transportation, price, inventory, processing, and terms of payment. Your total cost under each of the above options will be the costs associated with providing the same assurance of supply as under the original ordering method, plus transportation, price, terms, and processing cost. Unlike the transportation cost computed and applied in Chapter 2, however, transportation under these options should be valued at the prime (lowest) rate available, since supply will be assured through stocking and there will be no need for premium transportation. Consequently, transportation costs for each alternative can be calculated either directly from the quote or through your traffic department's rate books, with no need for historical averaging. Price and terms of payment[1] can also be valued directly from the quote for each option, but inventory-cost valuation cannot be attacked in quite as direct a manner.

[1]Adjusted in accordance with the Chapter 2 procedure.

However, there is a common inventory link for all of the above options that allows relative inventory valuation. This common denominator is the safety stock that you currently require to support variation in demand. Your safety stock has been computed and established in order to guard against extreme demands. Those alternatives that do not require the vendor to maintain a stock level greater than your existing safety stock will demand that you carry a buffer stock of your own to supplement the protection provided by the vendor.

The following formula will enable you to value this supplement stock relative to price.

Equation 7

$$\frac{\text{Supplementary}}{\text{Inventory Cost}} = \frac{(SS - RQ) \times (h) \times (p)}{\text{Annual Value of Commodity}}$$

where: SS = your existing safety-stock level in number of units.

RQ = release quantity under each option expressed in number of units.

h = your holding cost

p = old price per unit or new price if lower

If the result is negative, you are receiving sufficient protection to eliminate your safety-stock inventory. If positive, the cost should be added to the price of the alternative under investigation.

Processing costs under each alternative also must be valued relative to price. Since even under a "paperless order system" such as dataphone you still must incur the costs of receiving, moving, and accounting for the material, your processing savings amount only to the cost of those activities no longer required. This type of contracting can result in order-processing costs being cut in half. Mechanisms for accomplishing such a reduction are dataphone, telephone releasing or multipart form sets. These mechanisms are conducive to this type of contracting since they can be used effectively with the prescheduled release quantities inherent in systems contracting. In relation to this type of systems contract, if these releasing alternatives are applied, processing costs should be valued as follows for each alternative:

Equation 8

$$\frac{\text{Order-Processing}}{\text{Costs Per Unit}} = \frac{(\text{Annual quantity}) \times (P.O.)}{2\,RQ}$$

where: RQ = release quantity under each option

PO = purchase-order processing cost

After computing the above costs for each alternative and selecting the lowest-cost alternative, compare this cost to that for the present ordering method to identify if a change is recommended and to determine the savings available. Then negotiate in order to insure that your decision will be effective for the duration of the contract.

In order to determine if additional forecast detail would be desirable, you may proceed through the following steps. The minimum value available for additional forecast detail can be estimated based on the cost of the additional safety stock required under the lowest-cost alternative. If this value appears significant, review forecasting methods in Appendix 10 and determine if it is significant enough to justify greater forecast detail in order to eliminate safety-stock requirements and reduce total costs even further.

REDESIGN

As in make-or-buy, the value of purchasing participation in a design-or-redesign program is purchasing's contact with the marketplace and the accompanying ability to call on many vendor-commodity engineering specialists to identify the optimum specification for the function required. In many firms, purchasing participation in these activities would be considered usurping the design prerogative of engineering. Purchasing, however, is not a design group and is in no way equipped to handle this responsibility. With respect to redesign activities, purchasing serves as a coordinator of a vendor-design review with engineering controlling the final design selection based on its responsibility for integrity of product.

The overview to this chapter recommended a means for identifying those commodities for which you should initiate a redesign activity. This recommendation instructed that the redesign approach should be applied to your highest-cost commodities for which price and quality costs represented the highest cost-element combination. The logic behind this suggestion becomes clearer in reviewing typical applications of respecification. These applications were identified as:

1. *Change to industry standard:* tolerance, design, production-processing procedures, and specification.
2. *Substitution of material:* functional substitution and change to company standard.

In all of these applications, you are searching for the optimum specification, one that will meet your operating and quality requirements at the lowest possible costs. As we have discussed, these costs have two components. The first is the cost of sufficient quality. This cost is contained in the price. The second is the cost of insufficient quality, which is the quality cost associated with claims and late delivery and is not reflected in the price.

Both of these costs are significantly affected by the engineering specification, since it is this factor that identifies the type of material, the manufacturing process for which the vendor must incur costs, and the probability (as a result of specification exactness) that the vendor will not be able to meet the specifications required. Thus, redesign provides the greatest potential for cost reduction of commodities that are highest in these two cost areas.

However, this keying technique provides just one of many avenues into a redesign project. Often, significant opportunities will be identified through vendor suggestions, your own commodity knowledge, and new product developments. Further, it will be to your advantage to provide the opportunity for your vendors to utilize their design capability on practically everything you buy through the use of a specification identifying what you need rather than what is already designed. The trick to applying this technique is to be able to determine how probable redesign is for a given commodity, before you invest a lot of your time or your vendor's in drastically changing the design of a small-value purchase for which the savings will not come near the cost of drawing changes and necessary modifications in interfacing equipment. To determine this, it is first necessary to identify the specification options: competitive, competitive-performance, and design, and to describe how to determine when each of these specifications applies to any particular commodity.

Competitive Specification

The competitive specification is the most common form of commodity description used in industry today. This specification describes the commodity without using vendor style numbers or brands to hide actual requirements. Components of this type of specification can be displayed as follows for common commodity groupings (in this type of specification the detail shown below is unnecessary only if there is an industry-recognized style number that can replace these specifics).

1. Specifications for raw material, fabricated parts, castings and forgings, and other commodities designed by you should include:
    a. General commodity description (i.e., plate, forging, etc.)
    b. Dimensional drawing and acceptable tolerances (or equivalent)

    c. Material specifications

    d. Special fabrication or process instructions

    e. Acceptance criteria

        1) Tests that must be conducted by vendor and your company and necessary reports

        2) Sampling procedure

        3) Point of inspection

        4) Other

2. Specifications for mechanical, hydraulic, electrical commodities and other material designed by others should include:

    a. General commodity description (i.e., value, motor, resistors, etc.)

    b. Envelope drawing with maximum dimensions and minimum dimensions for connections to interfacing equipment.

    c. Input parameters (e.g., Input:

                    Valve = characteristics of inlet flow

                 Motor = characteristics of electricity inflow

        Speed Reducer = force characteristics)

    d. Material specifications

    e. Identification of special provisions necessary as a result of external pressure, temperature, and atmosphere of significance to equipment's operation.

    f. Performance parameters

        1) Duty cycle and necessary life

        2) Output parameters required (e.g.,

            Motor = torque and speed characteristics

            Pump = flow, head)

        3) Code restrictions on performance (e.g., OSHA, etc.)

    g. Acceptance criteria (see above)

As you can see, there is a distinct difference in the way you must specify equipment designed by your company compared to that designed by your vendors since you are not free to transmit vendor drawings for competitive bid. Even if you were, the vendor receiving a competitor's drawing would be at a decided disadvantage in quoting, since he would not have access to all the design parameters that went into the original vendor's selection.

The inquiry structure that will enable you to determine if there are redesign opportunities consists of encouraging vendors to suggest beneficial alternatives by requesting them to quote "as specified" and also to quote alternates with lower-cost tolerances, radiuses, and material specifications of equal properties. Later in this chapter we will discuss the method for identifying whether a vendor-suggested alternate presents a significant enough cost advantage to pursue.

Competitive-Performance Specification

The competitive-performance specification differs from the competitive specification only for equipment that has been designed by your company (Category 1 above) and is applicable only when you would find it desirable to transfer performance responsibility for this equipment to your vendor, or when you have identified that there may be a cost advantage in redesign and wish to use your vendor's capabilities in this effort. As you may have inferred, this specification is nearly identical to the type used for the competitive specification of vendor-designed equipment except that it states both your existing design result and design parameters. The composition of this specification is as follows:

1. Existing Design
   a. General commodity description
   b. Dimensional drawing and acceptable tolerances marked to display maximum envelope dimensions and identifying corrections
   c. Material specification
   d. Special fabrication-process histories
2. Design Parameters
   a. Input parameters[1]
   b. Description of limiting external environment (e.g., corrosive atmosphere, moisture, etc.)
   c. Dimensional interface drawing (schematic showing necessary interfaces with connecting equipment)
   d. Output parameters
      1) Duty cycle (continuous-noncontinuous operation at designated intervals)
      2) Life required
      3) Form and dimensions of required output
      4) Environmental restricting on output (such as OSHA)
      5) Acceptance criteria (description of); Tests; Measurements; Counts; Other

For this specification, you should request that vendors quote a commodity that will meet the existing design and also quote an alternate in

---

[1]For a motor, input would consist of electrical parameters. For a container, input would be parameters of medium to be contained. For a supportive device (base plate, etc.) input would be the force that this commodity is subjected to.

accordance with the given design parameters. Through this approach you not only enable a vendor to use his engineering creativity in determining a suitable alternate, but you also can assure vendor responsibility for the commodity meeting the necessary design specifications. As you can see, the competitive-performance specification provides a great deal more latitude in allowing the vendor to apply his knowledge to assist in the selection of optimum specifications.

Design or Functional Specification

The design specification is applicable to the major redesign projects that you have identified and to high-cost, initial-design projects. It is the most expensive approach of the three, but also provides the fewest creative restrictions on your vendors' design departments and, thus, offers the greatest possibility of a high return for your effort.

The key requirements to effective design activities are a broad functional specification and a method for identifying which vendors are capable of supplying these functional requirements. Briefly, the functional specification should describe input available (rather than selected input as in the other specifications), surrounding environment, and output required to perform the function. With this type of description, you can allow a vendor's engineering department to look beyond surface-design revisions and concentrate on the best possible design to meet your situation and needs. As an example of the value of this approach, in the other specifications, if a power source was necessary to meet a functional requirement you would identify the specific type of power source selected, such as an electric motor, and ask the vendor to suggest the best motor for your situation. However, by doing this, you have automatically eliminated diesels, turbines, and others from your review even though gasoline, oil, or steam may be readily available to serve as inputs and much more economical. To avoid this channeling, this specification requests identification of:

    I.   Input available — referring to the types of energy, classifications, and ratings available to make the commodity react. Within this classification would be energy sources such as:
        A.   Coal
        B.   Gases
        C.   Petroleum
        D.   Nuclear
        E.   Mechanical
        F.   Chemical
        G.   Thermal

    H. Electricity
    I. Manual
    J. Hydraulic
    K. Light

II. Constraining environment — describing the limiting-design environment in which the work will take place, both internal and external to the reaction.
    A. Atmosphere
        1. Chemical
        2. Moisture
        3. Temperature
        4. Dust
        5. Light
        6. Ventilation
        7. Natural disturbances
        8. Pressure
        9. Altitude
    B. Spacial arrangements
        1. Space available (maximum dimensions)
        2. Minimum dimensions

III. Output required — including a functional description of the work to be accomplished and how acceptance will be determined.
    A. General description of primary function (e.g., create force)
    B. Output parameters
        1. Duty requirements
           a. Duty cycle
           b. Life
        2. Form and parameters of output requirements
           a. Chemical
           b. Thermal-heat transfer
           c. Electrical
           d. Physical properties
           e. Mechanical
           f. Hydraulic
           g. Production considerations
           h. Appearance
           i. Tolerance
    C. Environmental restrictions on output such as OSHA.
    D. Acceptance criteria
        1. Tests
        2. Measurements
        3. Count
        4. Other

To assist in your application of this type of specification, it will be worthwhile to subclassify commodities into one of the following groupings before proceeding: reactive, containment, or supportive.

These groupings may be defined and related to the criteria as follows. Reactive devices are those that convert the input into an alternate form of energy. For instance, a motor, lathe, fan, or drive shaft changes the form or direction of input energy into a required output. Therefore, in specifying these commodities it is necessary to describe the energy sources available (at the job site), the limiting environment in which the conversion must take place and for which the equipment must be designed, and the desired output required, in terms of the end product desired and the maximum effect of the reaction on the environment (as governed by safety or code requirements such as OSHA). Consequently, when specifying a reactive commodity, you will end up with a long list of available energy sources and parameters of these sources, providing numerous vendor-industry options.

Unlike reactive commodities, containment devices must restrict the input energy in a constrained manner rather than converting it. For example, a hose, tube, or even reactor vessel must be able to restrict the flow of fluid but not contaminate this input. Consequently, for containment commodities there is only one important input that must be precisely described. However, the method of restricting it is left to your vendor's ingenuity.

The description of the containment function will be similar whether your input is fluid, gas, light, or electricity. The external environment is described in the same manner as in the reactive commodities, but the containment-output criteria will involve primarily the physical properties, duty cycle, and maximum chemical reaction to the input. For instance, if a fluid is the contained input, certain flow, pressure, and purity must be maintained and should be specified as the output criteria.

Finally, the supportive commodity is one that physically supports a containment or reactive device. The input of concern will, in most cases, be mechanical (friction, vibration, etc.). The environment will affect the support provided (corrosion, etc.) and therefore must be described, and necessary output will be identified primarily in terms of the physical, mechanical, and output-environmental factors.

Application (Vendor Selection)

Providing a complete set of specifications to enable a vendor to quote with respect to function without constraint to the actual selection of the product line has obvious advantages. First, you are using vendor manufacturing design and application. Second, you can establish vendor responsibility for performance. Third, you increase vendor competition and effort through providing a variety of functional alternatives.

However, selecting the proper vendors to quote a broad functional specification, for instance where reactive input may take many forms, requires some forethought. This is unlike the competitive and competitive-performance specifications, in which the identified input and output requirements determine which industry to ask, thus requiring only a search of your past procurement sources or the *Thomas Register* for this industry. The design specification, by leaving the input type of equipment optional, allows a great deal of choice as to which vendors should receive the inquiry. The most direct method of obtaining information about vendors capable of supplying your functional requirements is to create a vendor-functional library, to subcategorize vendor products supplied to you by cost related to their functional parameters. In this way, you will have at your fingertips all of your existing vendors and potential new sources classified by the input parameters that the vendor's equipment can utilize to provide desired output, the cost to meet the functional requirements, and constraining environmental conditions under which the vendors' equipment can function effectively. Identifying vendors of potential importance to your investigation, with this listing available, would simply involve selecting those vendors whose products matched the specification under review at the least cost.

If for any reason such a file cannot be created, less encompassing alternate methods may be applied, such as the use of published key-function cost lists. A key-function list such as that in Chapter 11 of G. W. Aljian's *Purchasing Handbook* (1966) can identify vendor industries capable of providing economical functional equivalents. On reviewing these equivalents and identifying those of value, you could then go to your own vendor files or references such as the *Thomas Register* to select vendors by industry that should receive inquiries with respect to your functional specification. The benefit in creating your own file as opposed to using published data is that your data will precisely fit your situation. The costs will be those you have actually paid for doing business with vendors and industries. The published data, although costing nothing to collect, will not be as complete as your own data and will be based on averages rather than actuals. Thus, published information will not yield as precise as a result.

Regardless of the direction you choose, the industry identification process can be utilized as follows. As an example, let us assume that you are investigating a "containing" function, perhaps a small vessel, and that your function list identifies that only plastic and steel can perform the function required at the cost as related to output parameters. (See Figure 10.) Through this analysis it is easy to see that the prime alterna-

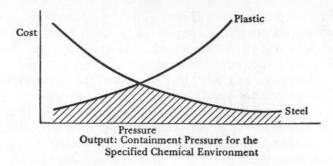

FIGURE 10.   Cost-Function Analysis

tive below given-output requirements is plastic, whereas steel is lower in cost above this requirement. Consequently, your inquiries would be best directed towards the lowest-cost alternative related to the specific functional parameters required.

In conjunction with this approach, a display on your premises of your key respecification projects describing the intent of the display, your objective (lowest total cost), and the functional requirements of the commodity would serve not only to inform vendors of your desire to investigate respecification approaches on these commodities, but also to remind them visually of your commitment to improve performance.

Target Improvement

Once you have selected vendors for bids, issued inquiries, and received their quotations, it is necessary to identity which offers are attractive enough to pursue. This requires identifying an anticipated yield and comparing the yield to change-over costs (investment analysis). Before instituting this investment analysis, however, it is first necessary to decide if the offers you have received are representative of the lowest cost required to perform the function. This can be done through relating the offers to an escalated version of the cost-function relationships that you used to select vendors for inquiry. To illustrate this analysis, Figure 11 uses the sample cost-function relationship in Figure 10 and an assumed cost of offers that have been received.

Obviously, in this situation Offer C constitutes the best offer received, but it is still above the escalated cost-function level that we have been able to achieve in the past. There could be any number of reasons for this occurrence: an over-cautious vendor escalation estimate, vendor failure to identify optimum production methods, or misunderstanding regard-

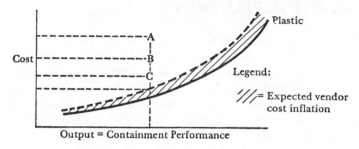

FIGURE 11.   Functional Target Pricing

ing your actual functional requirements. Regardless of the cause, however, it will behoove you to hold additional conversation with Vendor C before conducting your investment analysis, in order to identify the lowest possible cost available.

Once this review is completed, you should then conduct an investment analysis to determine if the necessary investment in both potential capital outlays and change-over expense (such as drawing revisions, etc.) is justified by the available return. This analysis should proceed as follows:

1. Identify lowest cost vendor as described in Chapter 2.
2. If a cost-saving advantage exists through a change in specification:
   a. Identify magnitude of drawing or ordering process change-over costs in engineering.
   b. Identify if change will yield greater than a 30 percent[1] return on investment by dividing commodity savings for the expected life of the commodity by the change-over investment.

$$ROI = \frac{\left(\begin{array}{c}\text{Original}\\\text{price}\end{array}\right) - \left(\begin{array}{c}\text{Price if vendor}\\\text{is allowed deviations}\end{array}\right) \times \left(\begin{array}{c}\text{Expected}\\\text{usage}\end{array}\right)}{\text{Change-over Costs}}$$

3. Continue if *ROI* is equal or greater than 1.3. Stop if *ROI* is less than 1.3.
4. Recommend that engineering pursue redesign analyzed.
5. In contracting for this commodity, document the above specification to assure that the vendor is responsible for design and performance of equipment at the levels set by the specification.

---

[1]This necessary ROI should be predetermined by your financial officers.

NEW SOURCE DEVELOPMENT

We have already discussed routine new source development in Chapter 3. The keying approach to new source development differs in three important aspects: point of initiation, commodity identification, and potential vendor identification.

In the routine new source development, no activity was initiated until a new vendor walked in the door and indicated he was interested in your business. This action by the vendor also identified the candidate for new source development and the commodity (the highest-cost commodity that you procure in his line). However, in the keying approach, application is much more complicated; it requires that the buyer initiate the activity.

We have discussed in the technique selection section of this chapter how to identify prime-commodity targets for active pursuit of new sources. These were your highest-cost commodities that fell in a "sole source" classification. Consequently, we have guided the buyer to the commodity requiring new source development.

However, he still needs to know how to select vendors for inquiry. On the surface, this task appears easy, for it seems that he could simply refer to the *Thomas Register* or similar vendor directories to locate alternate vendors in the same industry as your current suppliers. But this search will only reveal vendors capable of manufacturing nearly the same design and specification that you are currently procuring. If alternate sources were this readily available for the current design, it is unlikely that this commodity would be in a sole source classification. And since this is one of your highest-cost commodities, it will pay to attempt to utilize the greatest amount of vendor capability in reviewing the requirements versus design of the commodity.

Therefore, it is recommended that the approach to active pursuit of new sources should be much like the preceding redesign application — in which you obtain a "design-functional description" of the commodity, select possible bidders through analysis of functional-cost relationships and vendor displays, and inquire using the functional specification. As you inquire, however, you will also find it valuable to include in the inquiry packet a vendor-qualification form like the one described in Appendix 9 to enable these new vendors to provide initial information describing their capability to reliably produce this commodity.

On receipt of the bids, you should review quotations to determine which vendor offered the least-cost alternative, including the preceding redesign, change-over cost analysis. If the vendor offering the lowest-cost proposal had not been previously qualified (is not on your approved vendor list for this type of work) but appears acceptable based on information provided on the completed qualification form, you should then arrange a physical audit of his facility; and finally, pending a favorable outcome to this audit, you would identify your negotiation target and negotiate as instructed in the Redesign section. In this way, you combine the search for alternate vendors with a design review, to enable you to get the greatest possible cost-improvement from your new source development effort.

SUMMARY

This chapter has identified efficient keying-improvement application approaches to make-or-buy, contracting, and respecification and new source development. A procedure was reviewed that will enable you, at minimal cost, to collect information necessary to identify your highest-improvement priority commodities and to determine which of these techniques offers the greatest return when applied to these commodities. Further, information requirements and decision approaches to each of these improvement techniques were delineated in step fashion in order to assure that buyers have the necessary structure to apply these decisions effectively and efficiently. Finally, techniques were described to enable the buyer to identify a negotiation target, to assure the greatest possible yield is obtained from each review.

≡5

Performance Evaluation— Goal Setting

Use of the preceding information and techniques will enable you to more effectively meet your lowest-cost objective. Obtaining and using the material-cost information in the manner discussed in Chapter 2 will enable you to minimize costs while performing the maintenance activities of vendor selection and expediting.

Applying the techniques in Chapter 3 will extend the scope of this minimization by facilitating effective use of the routine improvement activities: Combining and splitting requisitions, Escalation hedging, Quantity buying, and New source development. This will lead to the best decisions on the form of ordering, the quantity and timing of the order, and the adequacy of existing sources.

Chapter 4 broadens this quest for minimization even further to include the more difficult applications of the keying-improvement techniques: Respecification, Make-or-buy, Contracting, and New source development. These enable purchasing to contribute towards minimization by identifying the least-cost form of material, point of manufacture, and system for ordering material.

Figure 2 (see Chapter 1) summarizes these improvement cycles. But efficient minimization is also dependent on effective performance evaluation. Performance evaluation establishes the course for improvement by identifying where it is necessary, assists you in setting improvement objectives in order to build incentive to improve, and enables you to judge if your improvement course has been beneficial. This is the beginning (setting objectives) and end (evaluating against these objectives) for each of the activity loops that have been discussed.

Objective and Subjective Evaluation Required

Today, most purchasing evaluation systems rely entirely on subjective judgment. However, an objective evaluation system is required as well to enable you to realize the full potential of performance evaluation. Subjective evaluation and judgment will be required in any evaluation system. Even in a system based on objective measures, such as dollars saved, judgment is required in determining suitable measures and in appraising the applicability of a measure once it is decided on. But subjective evaluation does not eliminate the need for obtaining objective measures.

Use of measures such as savings, savings trends, and savings indexes, adds structure to subjective evaluation that facilitates constructive discussion with respect to current performance and need for improvement. Without such measures, effective review of how to improve performance is extremely difficult. Simply telling a man that he is good or bad without also providing the objective basis from which this opinion was derived serves little constructive purpose since you are not making available the information necessary to guide this man's development. In other words, without the structure afforded by objective measures, a great deal of the potential value of evaluation is lost since it cannot be transmitted. Consequently, subjective evaluation alone is insufficient to achieve the improvement potential of performance evaluation.

Performance Examples Insufficient

Specific examples of performance are one form of objective evaluation that could be used to supplement subjective judgment. However, examples are insufficient in obtaining the full value of a performance evaluation due to a potential lack of credibility. Examples can be biased or, if negative, interpreted as biased since they represent only a sample of performance. Further, example collection often leads to a "halo effect" in which one extremely good or bad example biases evaluation of all performance. To eliminate sample bias or inference of such, it is suggested that total performance measurement is preferable to example collection for providing the objective basis of evaluation. Let us now review the requirements of effective performance measures.

OBTAINING THE POTENTIAL OF PERFORMANCE EVALUATION

Obtaining efficiency relative to material-related cost, demands that you achieve the lowest total-cost mix for all of your commodities. Chapter 2 included methods to enable you to depict these material-related costs and their magnitudes. Further, Chapters 2, 3, and 4 discussed the techniques which, when applied, would result in material-related-cost minimization.

By converting the instructions in these chapters into operating procedures to provide the buyer with necessary cost information and decision direction, it is theoretically possible to assure that all potential minimization tactics would be pursued, applied, and reductions obtained efficiently. This theory, however, makes two very large assumptions. One is that the buyer has the time necessary for these applications and the other that he will take the initiative in applying the preceding techniques to assure obtaining all possible available yields.

In order to make sure that these assumptions do hold and that you will minimize costs, you must collect information that enables you to identify cost-improvements contributed by each buyer and apply the techniques described in the following sections to identify the relative value of these contributions and their relation to buyer load. The basic vehicle through which this information can be collected and displayed is an effective cost-reduction, reporting, and evaluation program.

Critical Program Requirements

Many cost-reduction programs and savings reports have received a poor reputation as incentive tools because of lack of reported savings credibility and no measurement of buyer's relative contributions.

Obviously, in order to generate incentive for a buyer to pursue cost improvement there has to be a reward for his participation. Too many programs in the past have failed to include this provision because of the above failings. Many programs have not been exacting enough to establish savings credibility. They do not assure that a buyer's reported savings represent the net savings contributed to the company and that they are the result of buyer effort rather than market windfalls. Thus, purchasing managers have been reluctant to reward a buyer for reported cost contributions.

Further adding to this reluctance is the second factor mentioned above: no measurement of buyer's relative contributions. Since purchasing managers have a limited budget, not everyone can get raises. Thus, the manager must be very careful to identify those who have been making the greatest contribution. Cost reduction contributions alone do not tell this story due to differing potentials on various commodities. To circumvent this problem, most managers subjectively weigh these contributions. Yet, when they do this, they dilute the incentive impact of the program by not adhering to contribution totals. Instead of this subjective insight, it would be desirable to include an objective relative weight within the context of the program to enforce program integrity and indicate to the buyer how and why his contributions will be weighed.

As a result of these observations, the program below includes the following provisions.

    I.   Credibility in savings provisions
        A.   Only net savings are reported
        B.   Contributions are capable of audit
        C.   Adjustments are made for factors outside of the buyer's control
           1.   Market conditions
           2.   Clerical load
           3.   Experience
   II.   Relative contributions
        A method is provided to distinguish relative improvement between buyers.

Cost-Reduction Reporting Procedure

Let us start this review with techniques to accomplish the objectives of net savings reporting and audit capability. To aid in meeting these goals, the following form and procedure are offered. As you will see, acceptable cost improvement activities for reporting are identified on Form 10 and briefly defined in the procedure. These activities, however, have already been discussed. They constitute a summary of the routine and keying improvement techniques that require a buyer's initiative and must be promoted through performance evaluation.

This form and procedure serve four basic purposes:

1. *Teaching.* It quickly identifies and reinforces desirable improvement activities for a buyer to apply.
2. *Audit.* It also assures that you will have all the information you require to audit his contributions to assure he follows the procedure.
3. *Net savings.* It forces the buyer's consideration of all material-related costs in reporting his contribution.
4. *Convenient reporting mechanism.* Finally, it provides a step-by-step reporting procedure to minimize documentation time.

Improvement Analysis

This cost-savings procedure enables cost improvements to be reported efficiently, but in order to use this data to determine buyer improvement and thus to lay the groundwork for your motivation program, you must first remove the effect of influences on these contributions that are beyond the buyer's control such as assigned commodity potential and buyer-commodity experience.

If you attempt to apply reported contributions alone as your performance evaluation criteria, you will find it almost impossible to determine if appreciation on deterioration in a buyer's contributions should have been expected due to:

1. Changes in clerical load leaving more or less time for buyer improvement applications.
2. Changes in vendor market conditions causing windfalls or losses of previously obtained benefits.
3. Changes in the level of total material costs for which this buyer is responsible increasing or decreasing his potential for improvement.
4. Changes in buyer-commodity experience increasing or decreasing the probability of achieving the same or greater improvement than that achieved historically.

or if these changes are actually the result of a different level of buyer effectiveness. Consequently, if you do not allow for adjustment of these factors within the context of your program, you will be forced either to deviate from the program results in your rewards or to administer rewards inequitably and by these actions seriously weaken the motivational impact of your program.

Therefore, in order to maintain credibility, it is necessary to adjust resulting savings levels for these influences. This adjustment can be accomplished through application of the following procedures which apply previously discussed information in a manner that enables you to first, remove the influence of a buyer's total material cost and delivery-delay potential through an indexing process akin to that applied in finance, in which changes in company profit are analyzed by indexing this profit with sales dollars; second, identify and remove the influence of clerical load and market condition changes; and finally, identify and remove the effect of the expected changes in performance that will result from changes in buyer-commodity experience through a learning-curve analysis similar to that applied in the make-or-buy procedure.

Instructions for Use of FORM 10

1. Complete upper part of form with names of the buyer or originator other contributor (s) and vendor (s) who contributed.

2. Complete middle left quarter of form to identify where savings was provided. Include all cost savings resulting from your improvement activity identified by the checked (√) boxes in category (a.) on right side of form.

3. Check applicable boxes in middle right quarter of form to describe:

    a. Which material related costs you affected
    b. Method applied in achieving cost improvement

4. Definition of Referenced Methods:

    Redesign — refers to:

    a. Design
    b. Standardization
    c. Redesign
    d. Tolerance change
    e. Substitution

    Quantity Discounts — refer to your suggestions leading to procuring at a higher quantity level to enable net cost reductions (balancing inventory vs. price savings).

    Make or Buy — refers to your suggestion and justification leading to change of our point of manufacture of a commodity from in-house to outside or the reverse.

    Contracting — refers to your suggestions leading to total cost reduction through term commitments either on volume or specific commodity requirements.

    Price Hedging — refers to your suggestions leading to ordering or shipping material earlier than required to save costs through avoiding price increases.

    Change in Order Method — refers to your suggestions relative to changing methods of ordering leading to savings in order processing costs.

    Negotiating — Self-explanatory.

    New Vendor — Self-explanatory

3. Explain your contribution in the lower half of form:

    a. Extent
    b. Initiation
    c. Participation
    d. Other comments to further describe project or identify additional purchase order and
       contract numbers.

Two alternatives are offered for your use in making these adjustments, the basic adjustment technique and statistical technique. The basic adjustment technique is simpler to apply but relies on structured, subjective judgment and the assumption that the percentage increase or decrease in a buyer's clerical load will be inversely proportional to his improvement contributions. In other words, if a buyer has only half the time available for improvement activities, he will normally be capable of yielding only 50 percent of the contributions achieved historically unless he improves his performance.

The statistical technique does not rely as heavily on judgment or require making the above assumption. Instead, it allows statistical analysis of results to determine the actual contribution, clerical load, and market-condition relationships that have been experienced before. Con-

FORM 10.

REPORT OF COST SAVINGS   Date: _____

BUYER'S *(OR)* ORIGINATOR'S NAME: _____

OTHER CONTRIBUTOR *(S)* TO SAVINGS PROJECT: _____

VENDOR *(S)* CONTRIBUTING TO COST SAVINGS PROJECT: _____

Commodity and/or project description: _____ _____ _____	**a.** Cost Category affected by improvement activity (Check applicable box): Cost Change $

a. Cost Category affected by improvement activity (Check applicable box):

		Cost Change $
☐	PRICE	$\pm$ _____
☐	INVENTORY	$\pm$ _____
☐	TRANSPORTATION	$\pm$ _____
☐	QUALITY	$\pm$ _____
☐	MANUFACTURING	$\pm$ _____
☐	TERMS AND CONDITIONS	$\pm$ _____
☐	ORDER COST	$\pm$ _____
☐	DELIVERY DELAY	$\pm$ _____

Purchase Order and contract numbers: _____ _____ _____

Old cost or delivery delay per unit: _____

Savings per unit: _____

Quantity on the above identified order (s): _____

Savings on the above identified order (s): _____

Annual commodity and/or project savings: _____

b. Method applied in cost improvement: (Check applicable box)

- ☐ REDESIGN
- ☐ QUANTITY DISCOUNT
- ☐ MAKE-OR-BUY
- ☐ CONTRACTING
- ☐ PRICE HEDGING
- ☐ CHANGE IN MODE OF ORDERING
- ☐ NEGOTIATION
- ☐ NEW VENDOR

ADDITIONAL COMMENTS OR EXPLANATION OF SAVINGS:

_____
_____
_____
_____
_____
_____
_____
_____
_____
_____
_____
_____

Submitted By: _____   Date: _____
              BUYER (OR) ORIGINATOR

Approved By: _____   Date: _____
             SECTION MANAGER (OR) SUPERVISOR

Approved By: _____   Date: _____
             PURCHASING MANAGER

sequently, results from this technique will be less prone to bias and will provide more accurate adjustments. However, you must be able to pay the price for these advantages because this analysis requires much more data to identify meaningful factors, is cumbersome without the aid of a computer, and cannot be applied unless you have a person available who is skilled in statistical analysis. For these reasons, it is suggested that all companies initiate the improvement analysis of buyer contributions using the basic adjustment technique that follows and apply the statistical technique only if capability is available and after sufficient data has been collected to obtain meaningful results.

Basic Adjustment Technique

The first step in the analysis of buyer contributions is to summarize these contributions in a form convenient to further analysis. For this purpose, page 1 of the "Buyer Improvement Analysis Form" (Form 11) is offered.

To use this form, record and analyze each buyer's contributions as follows: (Illustrations of each of these steps are provided on Form 11.)

1. In Column 1, enter the total-cost reductions and delivery-delay reductions that this buyer has submitted for each vendor industry with which he does business (e.g., forging, casting, steel, pump, etc.) and the techniques (escalation hedge, etc.) applied in achieving these reductions.[1]
2. Next, in Column 2, enter the total dollars purchased and the total delivery delays documented[2] for each of these vendor industries during the same period.
3. Now divide each figure in Column 1 by the respective total in Column 2 to find unadjusted percent improvement and enter the results in Column 3.
4. In Column 4, enter the results that you had obtained from the previous period for this industry (unadjusted percentage improvement).
5. Identify if changes in results between Columns 3 and 4 are caused by market conditions as follows:
    a. *Escalation Hedging:* Yields for this category will depend on the escalation in the industry in this period compared to last period. If prices have not gone up or have not increased as greatly as during the previous period, a drop in savings would be expected. Through your knowledge of the industry and a review of price indexes, it will be easy to determine if the change is due to market conditions or buyer performance and to put a check in Column 5 if market conditions are the cause for the change.

[1]Vendor industries and techniques can both be identified from the information displayed on the preceding "Cost Savings Form."

[2]This information is available on the "Vendor Performance Data Collection Form", Form 1.

FORM 11. Buyer Improvement Analysis Form

Vendor / Industry	1 This Periods Reductions — Cost	1 Deliv. Delay	2 Total Potential — $ Purch.	2 Deliv. Delay	3 Unadjusted % Improvement† — % Cost	3 Deliv. Delay	4 From Previous Period — % Cost	4 Deliv. Delay	5 Check If Change Due to Market Conditions*	6 Adjusted Results†† — Cost Red.	6 Deliv. Delay
Industry A		200 wks.	50,000	2000 wks	10%	10%		5%			100 wks
Escalation Hedge	1000				2%		3%		✓	1000	
Make-or-Buy	2000				4%		10%		✓	5000	
Negotiation	500				1%		1%			500	
Contracting	—								—		
New Vendor	—								—		
Balance	500				1%		2%		—	500	
									Total	7000	100 wks
Industry B											
Escalation Hedge											
Make-or-Buy											
Negotiation											
Contracting											
New Vendor											
Balance											

Buyer Name ___John Dor___   Period Reviewed From ___Jan. 1___ to ___Mar. 30___

†Divided respective Column 1 figures by Column 2 results to obtain figures for Column 3.

*Compare yields from previous period and current and review buyer attack to identify if increase or decrease is caused by market conditions.

††If checked, multiply Column 3 by Column 2 to determine market condition factor.

b. *Make-or-Buy and New Source Development:* Yields in this category will be affected by market load (industry capacity/production relationship). By reviewing the buyer's make-or-buy and new-source-development attack along with your knowledge of the marketplace, you will be able to determine if any drop or climb is due to his effort or changing market conditions. Again, if market conditions caused the change, put a check in Column 5.

c. *Negotiation and Contracting:* Here too, returns are affected by market conditions. Through review of buyer's attack and discussions with him, you will be able to determine if changes are due to market conditions or his effort. If the change has occurred due to market conditions, enter a check in Column 5.

d. *Balance:* The rest of the improvement techniques, *quantity-break*, *redesign*, and *change in mode of ordering* will be relatively insensitive to market conditions and, consequently, will not require adjustment.

6. Once you have reviewed these results in this manner, proceed as follows to adjust for market conditions.

a. For those categories checked, multiply the figure in Column 4 by the corresponding total in Column 2 and enter the result in Column 6.

b. For those categories without checks, transfer the corresponding contribution in Column 1 to Column 6.

c. Total these Column 6 entries for each vendor industry to display market adjusted totals.

This market condition adjustment is the most time-consuming of all the adjustments that will be made but does provide you a vehicle for keeping abreast of the market as well as gaining additional insight into the strength and weaknesses of each buyer's improvement attack and, consequently, will be very worthwhile. Once you have adjusted contributions for market conditions, transfer the adjusted totals to Column 1 on Form 12.

Next, adjust these totals for buyer experience as follows:

1. Estimate the period of time required for a buyer to become proficient in procurement within each vendor industry. (This estimate need only be made once and will be used again in subsequent evaluations.)

2. Find the number of months that the buyer has been procuring the commodity at the time of the review.

FORM 12.   Buyer Improvement Analysis Form

	1 *Market Adjusted* *Reductions*		*2*	*3* *Exp. Adjust.* *(1 – 2)*	
Vendor *Industry*	*Cost* *Reductions*	*Delivery* *Delays*	*Exp.* *Factor*	*Cost* *Reduction*	*Delivery* *Delay*
Industry A Industry B Industry C Etc.	7000	100 wks	.93	7527	108

Buyer Name_____ Period Reviewed From_____to_____

Answer 1 = Totals From Column 2, Form 11: $50,000 – 2000 wks

Clerical Load Factor: $\dfrac{\text{Maximum} - \text{Current Load}}{\text{Maximum} - \text{Previous Load}} = \dfrac{25\,200 - 12\,000}{25\,200 - 10\,000} = .9$

Adjusted Performance Level: $\dfrac{\text{Total Column 3}}{\text{Answer 1 (clerical load factor)}}$

$= \dfrac{7527}{50,000(.9)}$ Cost $= \dfrac{108}{2000(.9)}$ Delivery

3. Apply the curve in Figure 12 to determine the applicable experience-adjustment factor.
   a. Divide the number of months that the buyer has been handling the commodity by the months required to reach proficiency.
   (For example, assume buyer has been handling a commodity for three months and proficiency requires five months, your answer would be 3/5.)
   b. This fraction will locate the current buyer learning position with respect to the fractional distance between O and X on the months axis and thus will identify the expected buyer proficiency (in this example, 3/5 corresponds to a .93 proficiency).
   c. Enter this decimal in Column 2 for each vendor industry.
4. Then divide this factor for each industry by the respective figures in Column 1 to adjust for experience.

Once you have completed this experience adjustment it is necessary to adjust for changes in clerical load. After finding the clerical load[1] that each buyer has handled over this evaluation period, refer to the bottom of the above form, divide the (maximum load[2] minus current load) by the (maximum minus previous period's load) to find the clerical ad-

[1]Loads may be evaluated as described in Appendix 8.
[2]Total number of minutes of working time in the period.

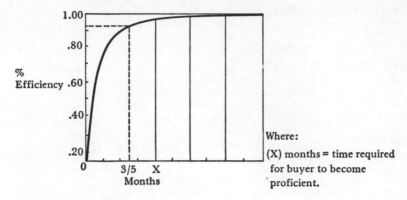

[1]This curve is the same Pareto or ABC curve reviewed in Appendix 5. It is used because it approximates the rapid building of knowledge in the early stages of development and the gradual leveling that you have actually experienced in training a buyer.

FIGURE 12. Performance Learning Curve[1]

justment factor and find the buyer's adjusted performance level by dividing the totals from Column 3 by the respective totals from Column 2, and divide each answer by the above adjustment factor.

This adjusted performance level provides an index of buyer improvement taking into account the effects of experience, market conditions, and load. By plotting this result from period to period you will be able to easily separate those buyers making constant improvements and, thus, more capable of handling increasingly responsible loads from those individuals deteriorating in performance.

Statistical Improvement Analysis

Now let us review a more detailed, statistical approach to performance evaluation. As indicated, this approach will yield more precise results, but does require a much more complicated analysis. The first step, as in the previous procedure, is information collection.

    I. *Information collection*

        All of the information designated below should be collected and totaled for the same time periods.

        A. *Identify cost-reduction contributions*

            1. Total the results submitted on the preceding Cost Savings Form for each buyer and Vendor Receiving Order combination.

2. Group these totals for each buyer by vendor industry to determine:
    a. Total dollar savings submitted by each buyer for each of his vendor industries.
    b. Total delivery-delay reduction submitted by each buyer for each of his vendor industries and enter on the following Statistical Improvement Analysis Form (Column 1).

B. *Identify total potential*
   Apply Chapter 2 material-related cost information collected on the Vendor Performance Data Collection Form.
   1. Total material-related costs for each buyer and significant vendor combination to determine:
       a. Total dollars spent by each buyer for each of his vendor industries.
           1) Price
           2) Freight
           3) Early shipment cost
           4) Claims cost
       b. Total delivery delays contributed
   2. Group these totals for each buyer by vendor industry and enter to the Statistical Improvement Analysis Form (Column 2).

C. *Clerical load*
   Apply Appendix 8 results (number and type of clerical documents processed) as follows to identify each buyer's clerical load.
   1. Total the number of each type of documents processed by each buyer.
   2. Apply (multiply) the time factors identified in Appendix 7 to the above count to determine total clerical processing time for each buyer in the past period. Enter this figure in Column 3.

D. *Market condition indicators*
   Identify the applicable market condition indicators for those significant industries identified above.
   1. For basic industries, identify the change in the production/capacity ratio that has occurred from the previous year-to-date by dividing the current year-to-date averages by that of the previous quarter.
   2. For other industries, identify the change in leadtime that has occurred using year-to-date averages as described above.

FORM 13.   Statistical Improvement Analysis

Vendor Industry	1 This Period's Contribution		2 Potential		3 Buyer Clerical Load (CC)	4 Market Condition Indicator (MC)	5 Experience Factor	6 Experience Adjust. $(1 \div 5)$		7 Expected Result Relationships*		8 Expected Results 2×7	
	Cost Red.	Deliv. Delay	$ Cost	Deliv. Delay				Cost Red.	Delay Red.	Cost Red.	Delay Red.	Cost Red.	Deliv. Delay
Industry A	8000	400 wks	100,000	5000 wks	300	.7	.93	8602	417 wks				
CR = 35 − 25 (MC) − .05 (CL)													
DD = 15 − 10 (MC) − .01 (CL)													
Industry B													

Buyer Name _____John Dor_____   Period Reviewed From ___Jan.1___ to ___Mar. 30___

Performance Level = $\dfrac{\text{Column 6 Totals}}{\text{Column 8 Totals}}$ = $\dfrac{\text{Cost Reduction}}{\text{Delivery Delay}}$

*Identify expected results by inserting Columns 3 & 4 into the equations referenced under each vendor industry and computing the result.

II. *Adjust contributions for buyer experience*
  A. Estimate the period of time required for a buyer to become proficient in procurement within each vendor industry.
  B. Identify the number of months that buyer had been procuring commodity at the time of the review.
  C. Apply the curve in Figure 12 to determine the applicable experience adjustment factor.
    1. Divide the number of months that the buyer has been handling the commodity by the months required to reach proficiency.
    2. This fraction will locate the current buyer learning position with respect to the fractional distance between O and X on the months axis. Enter the corresponding proficiency level in Column 5.
  D. Adjust contributions (Column 1) by multiplying each by the applicable experience factors in Column 5. Enter this result in Column 6.

This provides the basic data for this improvement analysis. Once you have collected a sufficient number of periods[1], process this information as follows to evaluate buyers' contributions.

  I. Apply multiple-regression analysis using the above information to identify the historical influence that has occurred in results performance due to clerical load and market conditions for each vendor industry. Accumulate the information listed below by vendor industry for as many periods as you have collected information.
  A. Identify total clerical load for each buyer responsible for the vendor industry under review.
  B. Identify the applicable market condition indicators for the same vendor industry.
  C. Also determine the applicable results-indexes for this vendor industry.
    1. Delivery delay adjusted for buyer experience.
    2. Cost-reduction dollars adjusted for buyer experience.
  II. Through multiple-regression analysis[2], identify the historical ef-

---

[1]In order for this result to be reliable, it is desirable that at least ten periods (quarters) of data be available. Consequently, initial results may have little meaning. However, if data collection is not initiated promptly, you will significantly delay obtaining these relationships.

[2]Generally, purchasing people will not have the necessary time or experience to determine these relationships. However, your sales or forecasting departments should be able to assist you in this area. This discussion is provided simply to outline the results you should expect.

fect of these buyer loads and market conditions on these industry results.

A.   Determine suitable multiple-regression relationships using
the above information for each industry-buyer combination. Display resulting formulas below each vendor industry
on the Statistical Improvement Analysis Form.

Example: Industry A – Buyer B:

$$CR = 35 - 25 \ (MC) \ .05 \ (CL)$$

Where: MC = Market-conditions index.
           CL = Total clerical load for buyer handling
industry under review for period
corresponding to market index.
           CR = Cost-reduction dollars index for data
corresponding to buyer industry under
review.

$$DD = 15 - 10 \ (MC) - .01 \ (CL)$$

Where: DD = Delivery-delay index for data corresponding to industry under review.

B.   As you apply this technique you should also identify the
standard error of forecast accompanying these regression
results (statistical approximation of expected variability
in CR, DD forecast) for use in the following relative
evaluation analysis.

Once you have determined these relationships, you are ready to find
buyer improvement by comparing expected results to actual results.
This can be accomplished as follows:

1.   Identify current results expected for each buyer's vendor industries by applying current market levels, clerical costs, and experience factors to these relationships. To do this:

    a.   Introduce responsible buyer's total clerical load and current
vendor-industry market index into each (DD and CR) result
equation and solve for expected DD and CR. (Refer to
example on following Statistical Analysis Form.)

    b.   Insert answers derived above into Column 7, expected re-
sults, on the analysis form.

    c.   Multiply each figure in Column 7 by the corresponding total
in Column 2 to find expected contributions at the existing

potential market and clerical load conditions and enter this result in Column 8.

2. Finally, identify the buyer's performance level by dividing Column 6 totals by those from Column 8 as instructed on the bottom of this form.

This performance level is applied in the same manner as in the basic technique. By charting performance levels, you will be able to see if the buyer has improved. Further, if you shift commodities, both techniques allow you to simply total a different set of expected vendor-industry contributions for each buyer in order to adjust your expected buyer results. Consequently, these approaches will be effective even in extreme commodity-rotation situations.

Relative Evaluations

An individual's or department's improvement in performance can be identified through trends of indexes and the adjustments described above. However, comparison of improvement between individuals or departments is not so readily achieved because of the inability to rank absolute difficulty between commodity areas.

Yet, without the ability to make relative comparisons, it is impossible to determine if buyer A's 5 percent cost-reduction improvement is better or worse than buyer B's 10 percent cost-reduction improvement; and consequently, you cannot achieve the full incentive value of evaluation. Publicizing these results is important to motivation, but publishing results prompts comparison. Avoiding inaccurate negative comparisons necessitates having measurements that are comparable.

To provide this relative measure, it is suggested that you depict the likelihood of a specific performance index being achieved as a percentage derived from historical performance analysis in each commodity or group of commodities. This percentage, because it is relative to past performance within each commodity classification, will account for difficulty differences as experienced historically and, thus, will enable comparisons.

As in improvement evaluation, two techniques will be offered to enable you to depict relative improvement between buyers. Both convert the improvement measure to a percentage and both can be applied regardless of whether you selected the basic or statistical improvement-evaluation approach. However, the technique immediately following requires only simple arithmetic whereas the other requires statistical analysis and is much more time-consuming. Advantages and disadvan-

FIGURE 13. Statistical Improvement Analysis

Vendor Industry	1 This Period's Contribution		2 Potential		3 Buyer Clerical Load (CC)	4 Market Condition Indicator (MC)	5 Experience Factor	6 Experience Adjust. (1 ÷ 5)		7 Expected Result Relationships[1]		8 Expected Results 2 X 7	
	Cost Red.	Deliv. Delay	$ Cost	Deliv. Delay				Cost Red.	Delay Red.	Cost Red.	Delay Red.	Cost Red.	Deliv. Delay
Industry A													
CR = 35 – 25(MC) – .05 (CL)	8000	400 wks	100,000	5000 wks	300	.7	.93	8602	417 wks	2.5%	5.0%	2500	250
DD = 5 – 10(MC) – .01 (CL)													
Industry B													

$$CR = 35 - 25(.7) - .05(300) = 2.5\%$$
$$DD = 5 - 10(.7) - .01(300) = 5.0\%$$

Buyer Name John Dor   Period Reviewed From Jan. 1 to Mar. 30

Performance Level = $\dfrac{\text{Column 6 Totals}}{\text{Column 8 Totals}}$ = Cost Reduction $\dfrac{8602}{2500}$ = 3.4   Delivery Delay $\dfrac{417}{250}$ = 1.7

[1] Identify expected results by inserting Columns 3 and 4 into the equations referenced under each vendor industry and computing the result.

tages will be discussed with the presentation of each technique to enable you to choose the one preferable for your operation.

Basic Relative Evaluation

To apply this method, you need only identify the average historical performance level obtained in those vendor industries for which each buyer is responsible and divide this average into the buyer's current performance level to find percentage of improvement.

Since this percentage is based on past vendor-industry performance and represents the improvement that each buyer has contributed to your department's performance in these industries, this measure will provide an effective, relative measure of improvement between buyers.

However, use of this measure requires that you accept the fact that the absolute differences in the resulting measures between buyers will not necessarily reflect improvement effort put forth by each buyer. As an example, if one buyer's rating is 80 percent and another's 60 percent, this will not mean that the 80 percent buyer is 33⅓ percent better than the second buyer or that he has necessarily worked harder to achieve this level. The reason that this conclusion is invalid is that it may be much more difficult to improve performance in certain commodities than in others. To compensate for this degree of difficulty, apply the statistical technique that follows.

Statistical Relative Evaluation

The degree of difficulty can be shown by using historical information and a probability distribution. For example, the curve in the accompanying graph represents a buyer's performance index and shows the number of times that a range of performance levels has been achieved historically. The effect of clerical load and market conditions has been removed from this data so the curve represents only buyer-effectiveness.

From the curve, it can easily be seen that average performance would be 5 percent and that levels between 4 and 6 percent were more frequently obtained than those less than 4 percent or more than 6 percent. In other words, the curve indicates that it has been more difficult for the buyer to achieve a 9 percent rating than a 6 percent rating since 6 percent occurs more often. With the same logic, it has been more likely for the buyer to drop to a 4 percent rating than a 2 percent rating.

By sampling indexes over time, it is possible to establish this likelihood of occurrence through statistical analysis. This was done when you computed the standard error of forecast for each of your vendor industries in the statistical buyer-improvement analysis. By totaling standard errors

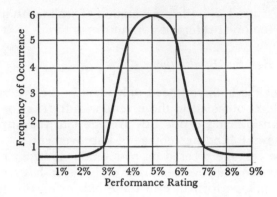

FIGURE 14.   Probability Distribution of Performance Occurrence

for all of a buyer's vendor industries and multiplying by $\sqrt{n}/n$, where n equals the number of vendor industries for each buyer, you can compute the sample standard error of forecast that is applicable to each individual buyer.

By displaying actual performance in relation to average performance, improvement between individuals or departments can be compared because the degree of efficiency is equalized through relative percentages. In reviewing this whole process, let us assume that a buyer submitted $10,000 in cost reductions during a given period and purchased $100,000 worth of material. His cost-reduction index then would be 10 percent.

If we assume further that the market condition was rated on the basis of the production/capacity ratio at 70 percent and clerical load identified as 100 units, cost reductions would then have been:

$$CR = 25 - (25)(.70) - .05(100)$$
$$CR = 2.5 \text{ percent}$$

Consequently, 7.5 percent (10 percent minus 2.5 percent) would be attributable to buyer effectiveness rather than market or load conditions.

Relative achievement could then be displayed for this period by relating the 7.5 percent to the historical degree of difficulty. If we assume that the average historical performance for these commodities was 5.5 percent and the standard error, 1.0 percent, his performance level would be:

$$\frac{7.5\% - 5.5\%}{1.0\%} = 2 \text{ standard errors or } 95\%$$

If another buyer had the same cost reduction figures but a standard error of 2 percent, he would have:

$$\frac{7.5\% - 5.5\%}{2.0\%} = 1 \text{ standard error or } 67\%$$

In this case, the standard error mean relationship indicates how likely it would be that a buyer would be at certain levels of achievement over or under the mean level. Therefore, performance is individual to the commodity but relatable to others' performance.

Consequently, with performance adjusted in this manner, a monthly publication or award program could be entered into by department or buyer to recognize significant improvers and to promote buyer and departmental awareness of performance.

SUMMARY

The proposed method for evaluating purchasing performance improvement reflects purchasing's contribution to profitability and is credible. Besides providing information that can be relayed regarding performance improvement, the system also provides guides to buyer relative performance efficiency and will assist in manpower planning and staffing justification. This method of indexes and analysis will assist purchasing managers in realizing the potential of performance evaluation by giving them a tool with which they can measure performance and the effect of external conditions on those results.

⬰ 6

Organization

We have now completed the review of techniques for achieving our primary objective, obtaining the lowest possible material-related-cost, but we must still discuss the method of identifying the organizational framework that will assure incurring the lowest possible administrative expense in realizing this objective. Without this guidance it is very easy to defeat our overall objective of lowest total cost, for without the proper number and application of buyers, you will reach this objective only by chance. Either improvement opportunities will be lost due to insufficient or improperly applied staff, or excessive administrative expense will be incurred. Therefore, in order to provide the tools to assure that the lowest total cost can be obtained, we must also define administrative decisions and identify approaches to insure efficiency in these decisions. To begin, let us delineate the three basic administrative decisions facing every purchasing manager:

1. *Commodity vs. product-line buying*. Should I organize buyers' responsibilities by assigning individual commodity responsibility to the fewest buyers possible, or by assigning each buyer a portion of my company's product line and all of the commodities falling therein?
2. *Centralized vs. decentralized organization*. Should I divide buying responsibility for commodities or products by having buyers at each using location (site), or have one site procure for all (multi-site)?
3. *Optimum size of staff*. After I have selected the most efficient organizational structure, how many buyers do I need to achieve the lowest total cost?

In order to insure that we can answer these questions we must discuss the necessary considerations to each question and how to determine which considerations are most important to your department.

COMMODITY VS. PRODUCT LINE

Overwhelmingly, purchasing managers have chosen commodity rather than product-line buying as the basis for their organizations. However, let us review why this is so and in what cases the product-line responsibility is more efficient. In this review, it will be beneficial to divide the discussion into two segments consisting of objective and subjective arguments for each type of organization. The objective arguments may be summarized as follows:

Comparative Objective Benefits

Commodity Responsibility	*Product-Line Responsibility*
1. Produces time savings in activities requiring vendor contact if common vendors are used in different product lines. a. Vendor interviews b. Vendor trips c. Expediting-proposals	1. Produces time savings in activities requiring engineering contact if engineers are divided by product line. a. Engineering interviews b. Personal visits c. Expediting
2. Produces greater vendor-commodity expertise.	2. Produces greater product expertise.
3. Facilitates consideration of total commodity volume in purchasing decisions.	3. Facilitates consideration of total commodity-product interface in purchasing decisions.

In analyzing these benefits, if there is minimum vendor overlap between your products, it would seem most efficient to organize by product line, since the commodity-responsibility benefits would be of much less significance than the product-line benefits. Conversely, if there is a great deal of vendor overlap between product lines, you will find it advantageous to divide responsibilities between buyers by commodity. We can justify this position very easily by reviewing each of the comparative benefits.

Time Savings

Commodity buying produces total time savings when you have an overlap of vendors between product lines. In this situation, if responsibility is divided by product line, you will have two or more buyers interviewing, visiting, and expediting or obtaining proposals from the same vendor. This undoubtedly will increase the total time expended in these activities because each buyer will take part in the introductory proceedings and travel necessary to conduct business with each vendor. On the other hand, the time required to deal with multiple engineers or internal personnel will not be as great as with a comparable number of vendors, since both your buyers and other internal personnel have similar objectives and thus will require less preparation for conducting business. Further, since it will also be typical that your internal personnel will be much more concentrated geographically than your vendors, travel requirements will be reduced through a commodity organization.

Expertise

Even more critical than time savings, however, is the consideration of expertise. Throughout this book two "golden rules" have been promoted: "Know Thy Vendor," and "Know Thy Product Application." If there is commodity similarity between product lines, it will be much easier to meet both of these conditions with a commodity-buying organization. As an illustration of this point, the similarity between commodity application in different product lines will be much greater than the similarity between the operations and processes of an electronics manufacturer compared to a steel supplier. Consequently, it will take much less time to develop a buyer familiar with one commodity's manufacture and the various product applications of that commodity, than the reverse.

Total-Cost Consideration

The final objective benefit stated that commodity buying facilitates consideration of the total commodity volume and relationships, whereas product-line procurement favors consideration of the commodity's effect on other commodities and product design. This consideration is factual but not of serious concern to this discussion because these advantages can be obtained through either organization via a coordinator. The purchasing-engineering position was created to serve this product-line overview purpose in a commodity organization just as negotiator positions (corporate, division, group, etc.) exist for the purpose of overviewing commodity-usage relationships between purchasing groups or buyers. Although a direct-buying responsibility facilitates performance of each of these functions, management leadership, in establishing cooperation with such coordinators, can eliminate a major portion of the additional benefit to be achieved through direct-buying control.

Subjective-Leadership Advantages

Although these objective benefits will point to the commodity organization in every situation but that with only a minimal overlap of vendors between product lines, some managers have adopted a product-buying organization because it assures accountability for getting a job done (shipping your product) whereas the commodity organization fragments this responsibility, and thus makes it more difficult to assure responsive performance. However, this justification not only ignores the fact that it may be less costly to your company to accept this disadvantage, but it also fails to consider that proper leadership (defining the response required and enforcing related disciplines) will enable you to have the best of both worlds. Consequently, before you give away these advantages you should define the parameters of responsiveness necessary to efficient operation in a commodity organization (such as maximum proposal turnaround, maximum requisition-placement time, claims-collection turnaround, and order-status transmittal and update procedures), and implement and enforce these disciplines within your organization. Only if this approach fails should you consider the product-line organization when the objective criteria dictate a commodity organization.

CENTRALIZED VS. DECENTRALIZED ORGANIZATION

Once you have selected either the commodity or product-line procurement, you must next, if you have more than one producing or engineering location, address whether it will be more efficient to centralize procurement or to allow a separate department at each location to procure their own requirements. These options are illustrated in Figure 15.

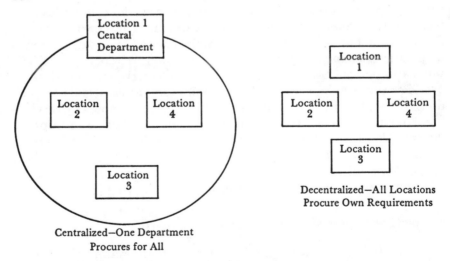

Centralized—One Department
Procures for All

Decentralized—All Locations
Procure Own Requirements

FIGURE 15.   Centralized vs. Decentralized Organization

In discussing the advantages and disadvantages of each of these options, it will be helpful to separate procurement activities into *contracting* (referring to vendor agreements based on consolidated volume concerning price, terms and conditions, delivery, etc.), and *buying* (referring to all other phases of procurement activities such as daily duties of source selection, physically placing the order, expediting, etc.).

This separation is necessary to divide activities into those dependent on and independent of the form of organization chosen. Contracting can be done through either line control in a centralized organization or through a coordinator in a decentralized operation. Thus, contracting and its inherent benefits are facilitated through centralized-line control, but can also be obtained with proper leadership (definition and enforcement of the coordinator's role) in decentralized organizations. Buying efficiencies, on the other hand, are entirely dependent on the organization chosen and thus form the crux of this decision.

Let us now investigate the important considerations in determining whether a centralized or decentralized organization offers the greatest benefits, with respect to specific commodities. These considerations are summarized below:

1. Is the dollar value high?
2. Is a long period of training required to become proficient in procurement of the commodity?
3. Is there a wide geographical separation between engineering departments?
4. Is there a limited number of suppliers capable of producing this requirement?
5. Are these vendors capable of supplying more than one operating site?
6. Is it necessary to set priorities for site demands with these vendors to assure supply?
7. Is there a wide geographical separation between manufacturing operations?

Obviously, the importance of each of these considerations to your efficiency depends on the specific type of commodity in question. Rather than discussing each of these relationships separately, the decision tree in Figure 16 is provided to identify and visually display the relative importance of each of these considerations through their sequence in the flow.

To illustrate the use and the logic behind this decision tree, let us proceed through each of the considerations displayed. The first question that must be answered with respect to the commodity being analyzed is,

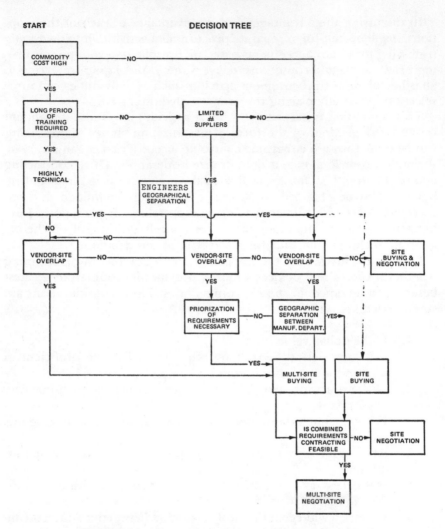

FIGURE 16.   Centralized–Decentralized Decision Tree

"Is the cost of this commodity high (one of those 10 percent of your commodities contributing 80 percent of your purchased dollars)?" If its cost is not high, you should favor decentralized (site) buying unless shops are in close proximity to one another. Further, you are advised to negotiate on a centralized basis only if:

   1.   There is an overlap of vendors between sites (vendor-site overlap), and

2. This type of negotiation is feasible (i.e., the commodity lends itself to combined contracting).

This route through the decision tree is illustrated in Figure 17 and can easily be justified, since the low dollar value is indicative that placing the buying near the shops to assure close contact will yield greater savings through emphasis on prompt delivery than the potential losses in the other material-related costs that you could incur as a result of spreading your expertise among a number of buying locations.

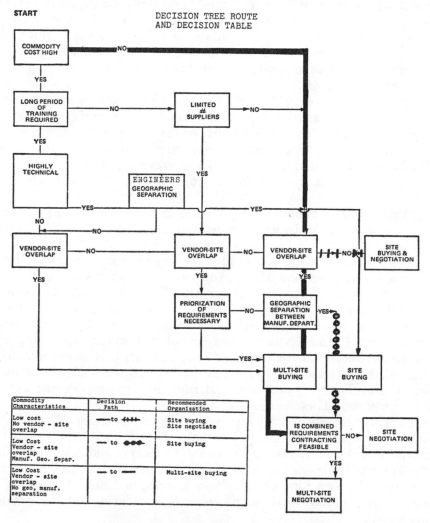

FIGURE 17.   Low Dollar Value Commodity

For a commodity contributing a great percentage of your cost, it is necessary to ask additional questions. First, "Is a long period of training (over one year) required to reach proficiency in procurement?" If the answer is no, you will not be overly concerned with the difficulty of developing expertise at multiple locations; but you still must make sure, in the event that there is a vendor-site overlap, that locations will not be harmfully competing for the capacity of a limited number of vendors.

If there is no overlap of suppliers, obviously, there is no use considering centralization. Further, even if there is an overlap, if suppliers are not limited or your volume compared to vendor capacity available is so slight that locations will not compete for capacity, the major buying concern will still be service to manufacturing. Consequently, in this case, you are returned to the question of geographical separation of manufacturing departments to determine whether you should consolidate buying or buy at the site.

However, if there are limited suppliers, vendor-site overlap, and the need for prioritization of requirements (such as during the steel allocations of the early 1970s), you are advised that multisite buying is preferable. In this case, closeness to manufacturing is of little concern if conflicting demands from locations will prevent assurance of supply. Each of these decision situations and conclusions is illustrated in Figure 18.

Finally, if the commodity is high in cost and requires a long period of training, an additional question must be asked, "Is the commodity highly technical?"

If it is not and there is a vendor overlap between sites, centralized buying is recommended. If it is, you must then ask, "Are engineering departments widely separated geographically?" If they are, engineering site buying is your only alternative, for as you have seen in previous chapters the engineering-purchasing-vendor interface is critical to cost improvement and efficiency, thus geographic proximity must swing the decision. However, if engineering departments are centralized or closely located, this interface can be maintained through a centralized or multisite procurement organization, and consequently this organization is recommended. These options are illustrated in Figure 19.

In applying these decision trees you can proceed through the decision shown for each commodity as we have done, or you may prefer to simplify application by using the summary recommendations shown in the lower left corner of each of the illustrations. With either approach, however, this structure will allow you to reach beneficial decisions and effectively illustrate the decision approach and conclusion to your management.

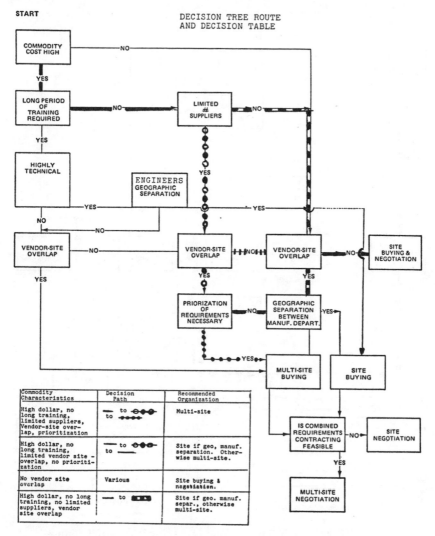

FIGURE 18.   High Cost Commodity—No Long Period of Training

OPTIMUM STAFF

Once you have set the responsibility patterns within your organization, you still need to determine the number of people that constitute the optimum staff. In doing this, you need to find out whether you have enough people not only for present activity, but for future activity.

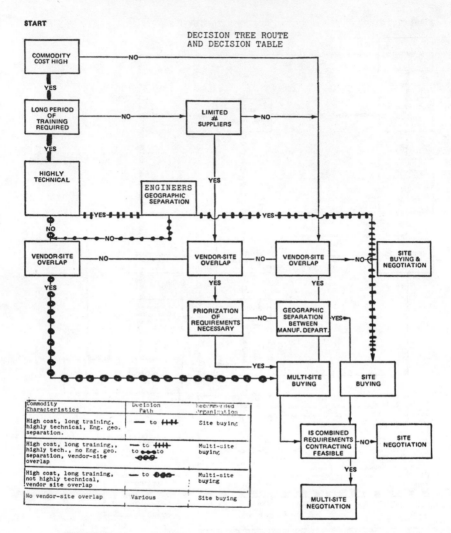

FIGURE 19.   High Cost Commodity, Long Period of Training

As was indicated previously, however, the decision cannot be made independently of material-related-cost efficiency. Instead, based on your objectives, you must discover what material-related-cost benefits or losses will be incurred through any staffing action, compared to the accompanying changes in administrative costs. Your intuitive experience will, in most cases, allow you to arrive at the staffing decision that will minimize both costs. However, it is often difficult to "sell" your decision to your management without having objective data available to support your recommendations.

In determining the specific form that this data should take we must, first, identify the relation of inadequate or excess staff to performance efficiency. As we have discussed, the improvement that you achieve as a department will be directly related to the time that you have available to devote to improvement activities. Further, by dividing purchasing activities into two categories, improvement and clerical, it is evident that it is essential to obtain the proper mix of clerical and improvement activity within your department in order to assure lowest-total-cost performance.

Fortunately, application of either of the techniques that were discussed in the preceding performance evaluation chapter will enable you to provide this assurance. If you will recall, one of the key adjustments for factors outside of a buyer's control is the clerical-load adjustment. In making this adjustment, factors were developed to identify the change in improvement performance that could be anticipated as a result of clerical-load changes.

With this prior identification of load (clerical) to yield (performance indexes), it is possible to identify how increases or decreases in buyer load will affect yield to assist in making effective staffing decisions. For example, using an assumed cost-reduction (CR) relationship and simplifying to show only the load-yield portion results in:

$$CR = .05 \ (C.L.)$$

Consequently, if you forecast an increase in load from 100 hours to 120 hours, this relationship identifies that this type of increase has historically resulted in a decrease in cost reductions of 1 percent (computed as follows):

$$CR = -.05 \ (120) = -6$$
$$\underline{\text{Minus } CR = +.05 \ (100) = +5}$$
$$\text{Net Decrease} \qquad\qquad +1$$

The question then becomes, "Will prevention of this reduction justify another man's salary?" This can easily be determined by comparing salary levels to the dollar effect of this 1 percent loss in cost efficiency. Thus, by combining the load-yield relationship with load forecasts, it is possible, as in this example, to forecast and justify necessary manpower requirements for efficient operation with respect to yield and salary trade-offs.

Further, by simulating varying loads with your existing staff with respect to these relationships, it is also possible to determine if you are currently at the optimum staffing level or if a staffing reduction or increase would produce a yield greater than the accompanying expense.

SUMMARY

Through application of these approaches, you will be able to reach efficient decisions with respect to commodity on product-line buying, centralized or decentralized responsibility, and optimum staff. As well, you have the tools available to lead your management through a visual display of these considerations, their relationships, and your conclusions in order to provide the justification for any decision you may reach.

Ξ Appendixes

$\equiv$ Appendix 1

DISCOUNT AND PAYMENT-DELAY TABLE MODIFICATION

To value additional terms for inclusion in this table or to revise this table for an alternate borrowing cost, simply follow the directions in the procedure below. To illustrate the application of this procedure, let us assume that you are interested in valuing the term 2 percent 10 net 90 and that your borrowing cost is 12 percent which is greater than the 10 percent used in computing Table 1.

1. First, determine the discount savings by applying the following formula (Omit this step if valuing a net payment term with no discount.):

$$\text{Discount Savings} = \frac{D\% + \left(\frac{IA}{360} \cdot D_d\right)}{100}$$

Where: $D\%$ = offered % discount
IA = company borrowing rate %
D_d = number of days in which payment must be made to receive discount

In this example since:

$$D\% = 2\%$$
$$IA = 12\%$$
$$D_d = 10 \text{ days}$$

$$\text{Discount Savings} = \frac{2\% + \left(\frac{12\%}{360} \times 10\right)}{100} = .023$$

2. Next, determine the Net Term Savings by applying the following formula:

$$\text{Net Terms Savings} = \frac{\frac{IA}{360} \cdot Nd}{100}$$

Where Nd = number of days in which the net payment is due

In this example since:
$$Nd = 90 \text{ days}$$
$$IA = 12\%$$

$$\text{Net Terms Savings} = \frac{12\% \times 90 \text{ days}}{100} = .03$$

3. Finally, identify which of the above provides a greater savings and complete Columns 2 and 3 as follows:
    a. The greatest savings should be entered in the "Relative Savings Column" (Column 2). In this example, .03 (Net Terms) provides your Column 2 answer.
    b. If this savings is provided by Net Terms Savings as in the above example, the discount is not worthwhile and "no" should be entered in Column 3; otherwise, enter "yes" in Column 3.

The preceding instructions will present little difficulty in valuing typical cash terms of the form 2/10 net 30. However, prox. or E.O.M. terms require additional explanation. These terms are used by manufacturers to indicate the day in the next month after material receipt in which payment is due. For example, 2% 10th prox. means that 2% may be taken if payment is made within 10 days of the first day of the month following billing. And 2% 10 days E.O.M. means that a 2% discount can be taken if payment is made within 10 days of the first day of the month following billing.

Therefore, if material was received on the 15th of the month (March, for instance) with 2/10 net 30 prox. terms, the discount payment would not be due until April 10, whereas with 2/10 net 30 terms payment would be due the 25th of March. As in this example, on the average, prox. or E.O.M. terms offer a payment delay of 15 days (one-half month) longer than the more usual 2/10 net 30 terms. This delay should be evaluated and the vendor credited for this benefit.

You can value the additional savings provided by a prox. or E.O.M. term by:

1. Computing the savings available from this "extra" 15 days:

$$15 \text{ day savings} = \frac{\frac{IA}{360} \times 15 \text{ days}}{100}$$

2. And adding this value to the savings you have computed (or that shown in Table 1) for the comparable standard term. For example:

To value 2% 10th Prox. Net 30
When $IA = 10\%$

   a. Compute value of the 15 day delay

$$15 \text{ day savings} = \frac{\frac{10}{360} \cdot 15}{100} = .004$$

   b. Add this savings to the comparable standard term, 2% 10 Net 30 (from Table 1) saves .023
   Therefore, 2% 10 Prox. Net 30 saves   .023
   $$\frac{+ .004}{.027}$$

$\equiv$ Appendix 2

VENDOR COST-IMPROVEMENT CONTRIBUTION REPORTING SYSTEM

In implementing a vendor cost-improvement reporting system, it is necessary to identify to the vendor the intent of your program and to provide instructions for his information submittal. This identification can be facilitated by use of a notification letter which includes descriptions of your intent, purpose, and use with respect to the information to be provided and concerning what will be allowed as a cost contribution.

The following letter and procedure have been designed to meet these objectives and are provided to aid in your rapid implementation of this type of program.

SAMPLE COST-IMPROVEMENT VENDOR-SELECTION LETTER

VENDOR: XYZ
ADDRESS:
ATTENTION: Tom Smith

SUBJECT: VENDOR SELECTION — COST-IMPROVEMENT
                CONTRIBUTION

We will be implementing an information system to assure that we include all material-related costs in our vendor-selection process. Recognizing that you, as our vendor, have a great opportunity to assist us in reducing our material-related costs, one of the primary factors in this system will be your cost reduction contribution.

We will look to you to report your cost-reduction contributions on a quarterly basis. You may report any contributions that reduce our total costs. Contributions should be reported on the attached form in accordance with the covering procedure.

155

Your reported contribution will be related to the dollars that we have purchased from you and utilized in vendor selection as an offset to your quoted price as follows:

$$\text{Net price} = (\text{Price}) - (\text{Price}) \frac{(\text{Contribution})}{\$ \text{ Purchases}}$$

We have implemented this system in order to insure that you get full credit for performance beneficial to our procurement activity and that this credit is reflected in actual vendor selection. Your comments, questions, or suggestions concerning this program will be appreciated and should be directed to the writer.

Very truly yours,

John Doe

VENDOR COST-IMPROVEMENT REPORTING INSTRUCTION

In using the attached form for your report:
I.   Complete upper left quarter of form to identify where savings were provided and the magnitude of savings.
II. Check applicable boxes in upper right quarter of form to describe:
A.   Which material-related costs you have effected
B.   Method applied in achieving cost improvement
1. *Redesign:* refers to suggestion or activity resulting in cost improvement from
a.   Design
b.   Standardization
c.   Redesign
d.   Tolerance change
e.   Substitution
2. *Quantity discounts:* Refers to your suggestions based on knowledge of production efficiencies leading to procuring at a higher quantity level to enable net-cost reductions (balancing inventory vs. price savings)
3. *Make or Buy:* Refers to your suggestions and justification leading to change of our point of manufacture of a commodity from in-house to outside or the reverse
4. *Contracting:* Refers to your suggestions leading to total cost reduction through term commitments either on volume or specific commodity requirements. This activity should enable you to balance your system efficiency against ours

5. *Advance notification of price increase:* There are benefits available to us through price hedging. Your contribution through advance notification will enable crediting of these benefits to your account
6. *Change in order method:* Refers to your suggestions relative to processing changes leading to greater combined efficiencies for both

III. Explain your contribution in the lower half of form:
    A.   Extent of participation
    B.   How you initiated

FORM 14.

Purchasing Department	*Vendor Report of Cost Savings*	*Date* _____

Purchase Order Number: _____

a. Category of Cost Improvement (check applicable box)

Purchase Order Date: _____	Price ☐
	Inventory ☐
Commodity: _____	Transportation ☐
	Quality ☐
Old Price Per Unit: _____	Manufacturing ☐
	Terms & Cond. ☐
New Price Per Unit: _____	Reliability of Delivery ☐

Savings Per Unit: _____

b. Method Applied in Cost Improvement (check applicable box)

Quantity ... This Order: _____	Respecification ☐
	Quantity Discount ☐
Savings ... This Order: _____	Make-or-Buy ☐
	Contracting ☐
Annual Savings ... This Commodity: _____	Advance Notification of Price Increase ☐
	Change in Ordering Method ☐
	Other ☐

Explanation of Savings: _____
_____
_____
_____
_____

Submitted by: _____
                        Vendor

$\equiv$Appendix 3

EARLY-SHIPMENT VALUATION

Since early shipment of material (before the required date) results in the necessity of carrying inventory longer than planned, there is a distinct inventory cost contributed by this delivery characteristic. With the information and technique that follow, it is possible to quantify this cost for both stock and purchase for contract material.

Cost Identification

The cost resulting from early shipments for a selected commodity grouping or vendor may be computed with the following formula and information:

Equation 9

$$\text{Early ship cost} = \sum_{x=1}^{x=n} \frac{I_A}{360} (D_x)(\$_x)$$

Where I_A = Interest charge
D_x = Days received early for each early shipment
$\$_x$ = Dollar value of each early shipment
X = Early shipment 1, 2, 3 ... n
n = Total number of early shipments per vendor

In this early-shipment inventory cost valuation the interest charge plus insurance and taxes is used to represent the applicable holding cost (I_A) since other common inventory cost factors such as space, labor, deterioration, and obsolescence will rarely be significant due to the relatively small holding periods involved in early shipments.

Application of the above formula enables you to compute the inventory holding cost incurred from early shipment. But application, without the aid of a computer, can be very time-consuming. Consequently, in the absence of computerization, it is suggested that the averaging approximation, below, be utilized to facilitate this valuation.

Equation 10

$$\text{Average early ship cost} = \frac{I_A}{52}(W)(\$)$$

Where: $\$$ = Dollar value of early shipment grouping
W = Average weeks received early for grouping
I_A = Applicable insurance, interest and tax charge per inventory dollar

This formula utilizes the information you have collected and prepared in your data-collection operation. Through application of this information and formula, you can compute an average early-shipment cost for the vendor being investigated. For instance, if $1,000 in material was received an average of four weeks early from Vendor A, the applicable early-ship cost would be:

$$\text{Early-Ship Cost} = \frac{.11^1}{52}(4)(\$1,000) = \$8.46$$

However, this computation can still be further simplified through use of Table 3, in Chapter 2. To use this precalculated table, find the applicable average weeks early for the vendor in question in column 1 and the corresponding cost in column 2. Then, multiply this cost times the value of material received early. If your applicable holding cost is different than 11%, convert this table by multiplying each number in column 2 by: Your Applicable % divided by (11%).

As an example, if we were to apply the table rather than the previous formula to find vendor A's early-shipment cost, we would initially refer to row 4 in the table to identify the applicable cost multiplier since material was received an average of four weeks early. As evidenced by the table, the multiplier referenced in this row is .00846 (column 2). By multiplying this value by the $1,000 value of material received early, you obtain: 0.00846 × $1,000 = $8.46. This is the same cost as that previously derived by applying the formula.

However, as is evident by the small value of the multiplier and the example result, unless early shipments are consistently very early, fre-

---

[1]Assuming that your company's (I_A) is 11 percent.

quent, and high in value, this cost adder will be very small compared to the other cost contributors and may not be worth the expense required for portrayal. Therefore, after computing this cost a few times for all vendors, you may wish to limit the early-shipment review to only a few of your consistently negligent vendors and further reduce the clerical expense associated with this technique.

$\bar{\equiv}$ Appendix 4

CLAIM-COST VALUATION

Direct costs incurred as a result of insufficient quality due to vendor error will result in a claim for recovery of these costs. If the claim value is accurate, the costs that you have incurred as a result of vendor error will eventually be recovered. Consequently, the claim represents a form of buyer-vendor trade credit. Assuming a valid claim exists, the effective direct cost incurred by the company as a result of vendor error is not the dollar value of the claim; instead, it is the financing charges necessary to support that claim value until it is collected.

In order to value the financing charges necessitated by claims, it is necessary to identify the dollar value of claims by vendor and the period outstanding for each claim. With this information and the aid of the following formula, you can value the vendor's claim-cost contribution.

Equation 11

$$\text{Claim cost} = \sum_{x=1}^{x=n} (C_x)\frac{I_A}{360} (D_x)$$

Where: C_x = dollar value of each outstanding claim
D_x = number of days each claim is outstanding
I_A = annual company borrowing cost
X = claim 1, 2, ... n for each vendor
n = total number of claims for each vendor

The formulation above, however, requires computing the interest cost of each claim that is outstanding. The method described below utilizes an averaging method to enable you to reduce computation requirements. The averaging method will not be as precise; but if computerization is not feasible, its use is recommended to reduce required clerical time.

The averaging formula associated with this method is:

Equation 12

$$\text{Average claim cost} = (C_T)\,\frac{I_A}{52}\,(W_A)$$

Where: C_T = total claims in dollars for the vendor or commodity grouping under investigation.

W_A = the average weeks for which the above grouping of claims is outstanding.

I_A = annual company borrowing cost

To further facilitate identification of claim costs, portions of this formula are precalculated in Table 4. To use this table, identify the average number of weeks for which claims have been outstanding for the vendor of interest and find this number in column 1. Column 2 of the same row contains the claims-cost factor. By multiplying this factor times the corresponding C_T (claims total), you will derive the same cost answer as that available through application of the above formula.

TABLE 4.   Claim Cost Factors @ 8% Borrowing Cost[1]

Weeks[2] *Outstanding*	*Claim Cost Factor*
1	0.0015
2	0.0030
3	0.0045
4	0.0060
5	0.0075
6	0.0090
7	0.0105
8	0.0120
9	0.0135
10	0.0150

[1]To revise table for alternate borrowing cost, multiply claim-cost factors by ratio below:

$$\frac{\text{Your Borrowing Cost}}{8\%}$$

[2]For a greater number of outstanding weeks than shown, multiply claim-cost factor by following ratio:

$$\frac{\text{Actual Weeks Outstanding}}{10} \times .015$$

$\equiv$Appendix 5

LEADTIME–LATE DELIVERY VALUATION

The following techniques are offered in order to simplify the inventory valuation of delivery characteristics and eliminate the necessity of detailed calculations.

These techniques are applicable only to material stocked for inventory. For material that is purchased to contract requirements, you are advised to apply the delivery-decision techniques referenced in Chapter 2.

Through application of the procedures and tables outlined below, you will be able to identify the cost of competing vendors' leadtime and unreliable-delivery characteristics for inclusion in your net-cost valuation and historical-cost ratio.

Leadtime Valuation

Many buyers tend to consider leadtime as a noncontributory cost factor. However, it is necessary to realize that the leadtime you obtain from your vendors will determine the replenishment stock levels necessary to minimize the total cost of both stock-outs and inventory holding costs; consequently, this factor does affect total material-related cost. In order to identify this inventory-cost effect it is necessary to review inventory decisions that are leadtime-related. These decisions are summarized by the following formula:

$$ORP = D_{LT} + SS_{LT}$$

Where: ORP = The inventory level at which a replenishment order should be issued
D_{LT} = Average demand within leadtime
SS_{LT} = Safety stock necessary to guard against uncertain demand within leadtime

In the event of certain or perfectly forecastable demand, the safety stock is not required and only the D_{LT} portion is applicable. In this instance leadtime has a negligible effect on stocking levels since the D_{LT} controls only the timing of the order, not the quantity of inventory on hand. (Discussion of the negligible effect is in Attachment 1 to this Appendix.)

Unfortunately, in most procurement situations, demand is not certain and safety stocks are required to guard against an exorbitant number of stock-outs. Elaboration of the safety stock portion of this computation results in the following formulation:

$$ORP = D_{LT} + ((SF)(S_d)\sqrt{LT}))$$

Where: SF = Statistical confidence factor
S_d = Standard deviation of demand (for period)
LT = Leadtime (expressed in demand periods)

Since the leadtime-inventory cost effect of D_{LT} is negligible, it is only necessary to consider the safety-stock portion of this formula in order to identify the inventory cost contributed by your leadtime.

To avoid repeating the computation associated with this formula, since much of the computation has already been done in order to identify your necessary inventory levels, Table 8 has been provided. With this table you can value your present leadtime and potential changes to this leadtime using available inventory information. In order to use this table to convert leadtime into cost figures, you need to know the safety-stock levels that currently exist in inventories for the commodities under investigation or for desired commodity groupings.

To assist in your understanding of this table, two application examples are presented below: cost of existing leadtime, and cost of leadtime change.

Cost of Existing Leadtime

To identify the cost of your existing leadtime (doing business with your current supplier), multiply your existing safety-stock level in dollars by the cost multiplier in row 10 column 3 of Table 8.

For illustration purposes, assume you have a

1. Total safety stock level for the commodity grouping of $1000
2. Holding cost of   15%

TABLE 8. Leadtime Valuation

New LT / Prev. LT	Safety-Stock Multiplier	Leadtime/ Safety-Stock Cost Multipler[1]
0.1	0.317	0.0475
0.2	0.448	0.0672
0.3	0.548	0.0822
0.4	0.632	0.0948
0.5	0.708	0.1062
0.6	0.776	0.1164
0.7	0.838	0.1257
0.8	0.895	0.1342
0.9	0.950	0.1425
1.0	1.000	0.1500
1.1	1.050	0.1575
1.2	1.097	0.1645
1.3	1.142	0.1713
1.4	1.186	0.1779
1.5	1.227	0.1840
1.6	1.267	0.1900
1.7	1.305	0.1957
1.8	1.344	0.2016
1.9	1.381	0.2071
2.0	1.415	0.2122
3.0	1.734	0.2601
4.0	2.000	0.3000

[1] Applies to a 15 percent holding cost. For alternate holding cost, recompute column 3 by multiplying your holding cost by column 2.

Row 10 in table 8, column 3 indicates that the cost factor reflected by your existing leadtime is .15. Thus, with the above safety-stock level, your annual leadtime cost is: (.15 × $1000 = $150 per year). This is the leadtime cost that should be included in your "hidden-cost ratio" for the vendor with whom you are currently doing business.

Cost of Leadtime Change

Using the figures from the example, if you enter a consignment program and your leadtime decreases to zero, you have saved the full $150 per year since a safety stock is no longer required.

If, however, a change to an alternate vendor would result in your leadtime decreasing or increasing, the table may again be applied to simplify valuation of the change. If we assume, for example, that the leadtime would double by ordering from this alternate vendor and the safety-stock level and holding cost are the same as in the above example, the leadtime cost multiplier would be displayed in Table 8, row 20 column 3. In this case, row 20 is applicable since the new leadtime divided by the previous leadtime is 2. Consequently, the applicable cost multiplier is contained in column 3, row 20 and is .2122. By multiplying this factor times the safety-stock level ($1,000), we find that the cost of the safety stock resulting from the new leadtime is $212.20.

Thus, on a competitive offering, a vendor that offered this longer leadtime compared to the original leadtime would have to present a sufficient price advantage to offset the $62.20 additional safety stock/ leadtime cost ($212.20 − $150 = $62.20).

Unreliable Delivery

In addition to the leadtime influence on inventory costs, unreliable leadtimes further increase material-related cost contributions. Valuation methods for unreliable leadtimes are presented below.

LATE-DELIVERY VALUATION (STOCK)

Late, unreliable deliveries will cause excessive stock-outs if inventory levels are not raised in order to guard against this influence. Since the influence of a potential unreliable delivery can be either a stock-out or increased inventory, two valuation methods are possible.

The most commonly discussed but least commonly applied method in heavy manufacturing is the valuation of a stock-out. However, although it is possible, it is extremely difficult and costly to attempt to approximate the stock-out cost for all your commodities. In addition, once this cost is calculated, it is highly likely that conditions such as workload shifts or planning changes will result in a meaningless stock-out cost structure unless substantial revision is undertaken.

A more realistic and equally logical approach to quantifying the cost of a potential late delivery is to identify the preventive cost of the excess stock-outs in terms of increasing inventory levels. In practice, this type of adjustment is made regularly by inventory personnel through inclusion of "water" (i.e., excess time) in safety-stock leadtime calculations to guard against leadtime unreliability, and it is this cost that is approximated below. In order to approximate the inventory reaction to unreliable delivery, however, it is first necessary to review the "expected stock-outs" that will be realized as a result of vendor's unreliability.

It is recognized by most purchasing people that late delivery, for example, in 1 out of 10 orders does not necessarily result in 1 out of 10 stock-outs and does not necessarily require the inventory reaction that a

10 percent stock-out level would because, in many instances, the material is not required immediately even when late. Less commonly realized is the reason behind the occurrence. It is natural in an uncertain demand situation that there will be times in which purchasing is forced to engage in expediting to assure a delivery, yet the material is not actually required for weeks or months. This is because planning for requirements with an uncertain demand necessitates anticipating an average or extreme demand during the replenishment period, even though a light demand is possible and would result in a material surplus. Consequently, in order to identify how much material must be stocked to prevent an out-of-stock, it is first necessary to estimate the potential of a stock-out in a given inventoried material.

Estimated Stock-outs

Table 9 expresses the probability relationship of an unplanned leadtime extension (vendor-delivery unreliability) resulting in a stock-out. The derivation of this table is explained in Attachment 2.

In short, however, by using the replenishment stock formula: $ORP = D_{LT} + SS_{LT}$. it is possible to identify what percentage of demands within the replenishment period are unprotected in the event of late-delivery leadtime extensions. This identification is the function of Table 9.

To illustrate the use of this table, let us assume that the commodity or commodity group you are investigating has the following vendor-delivery characteristics.

TABLE 9. Percent of Demands Jeopardized by Unplanned Late Delivery

D_{LT}/ORP	Average Late Leadtime / Planned Leadtime						
	1.1	1.2	1.3	1.4	1.5	2.0	3.0
0.90	38.3	83.5	94.5	95.0	95.0	95.0	95.0
0.80	12.4	33.2	60.0	72.6	86.0	95.0	95.0
0.70	6.9	16.2	28.4	41.4	53.7	88.9	95.0
0.60	4.2	9.7	16.5	24.0	31.9	66.9	92.0
0.50	2.9	6.5	10.6	15.3	20.1	45.0	77.9
0.40	2.2	4.7	7.5	10.4	13.6	29.8	57.4
0.30	1.7	3.5	5.4	7.5	10.7	20.1	39.4
0.20	1.3	2.7	4.2	5.6	6.9	14.2	27.0
0.10	1.1	2.1	3.2	4.2	5.2	10.2	18.0

D_{LT} = Average usage within leadtime

$ORP = D_{LT}$ + Safety Stock = replenishment stock

1. 10 percent of deliveries are late.
2. By an average of 2 weeks (12 weeks when late compared to 10 weeks standard leadtime).
3. Replenishment (ORP) stock composition
   a.   30 percent safety stock (SS_{LT})
   b.   70 percent average usage within leadtime (D_{LT})

Since $\dfrac{D_{LT}}{ORP} = 70$ percent, refer down column 1 to the .70 row and to the column headed by 1.2. This column is identified as applicable since:

$$\frac{\text{Average late leadtime}}{\text{Previous leadtime}} = \frac{12 \text{ weeks}}{10 \text{ weeks}} = 1.2$$

The tabled answer for row .7 and column 1.2 of 16.2 percent identifies the percentage of possible demands that are jeopardized by this leadtime extension. In other words in this situation, only 16.2 percent of all possible demands would result in stock-outs if the leadtime was extended by 20 percent with the existing safety stock.

Further, since only 10 percent of the orders issued have been overdue in the past, only 1.62 percent ($10\% \times 16.2\%$, the joint probability) received from this vendor will result in stock-outs due to this unreliable delivery.

In formalizing these steps to use this table to identify expected stock-outs:

1. Identify the relationship between D_{LT}/ORP.
2. Identify the average leadtime extension resulting from unreliable delivery by vendor/commodity or commodity groupings and compute the following ratio:

$$\frac{\text{Average late leadtime}}{\text{Planned leadtime}}$$

3. Find the result in the table to identify the percentage of demands jeopardized.
4. Identify the estimated resulting number of stock-outs by multiplying the result in (3) above by the percentage of orders overdue by vendor.

Expected Cost to Protect Against Stock-outs

Once you have identified the expected number of stock-outs, there are numerous methods that could be applied to cost this factor. A good summary of the available techniques is provided in M. J. Bronson, "The

Variable Leadtime Problem in Inventory Control: Survey of Literature, Part 1," *Operation Research Quarterly,* Volume 13, Issue 1.

However, to apply any of these techniques, it is necessary to more than triple the number of calculations used in most systems requiring *ORP* manipulation. This additional calculation is required since not only a demand analysis but also a leadtime probability distribution and interface analysis is necessary. Due to the necessity of a major time commitment for application of these techniques, an alternate approach, not as theoretically precise but sufficient to offer an approximation of protection cost, was investigated.

This technique involves using the same information required to identify "estimated stock-outs" to generate a "prevention" expected value. Table 10 displays the results. Derivation of this table may be found in Attachment 3. However, the approach may be summarized as follows.

The first column in Table 10 identifies the average-lateness (or leadtime-extension) factor for the overdue. The numbers in the column furthest to the right, headed by 100 percent, are cost multipliers for the necessary safety-stock additions based on the average late leadtime referenced and 100 percent of the orders being late. This column is based on a sound theoretical approximation of the safety stock required to prevent a higher stock-out level. For the other columns, however, the approximation deviates from sound theory. *ORP* theory indicates that in an uncertain-demand situation whether 100 percent of the orders or only 5 percent of the orders are late, since you cannot predict when the lateness will occur, it will be necessary to stock the equivalent of the full 100 percent safety-stock quantity in order to prevent an out-of-stock.

TABLE 10.   Expected Late-Delivery Valuation Factor (Safety-Stock Multiplier)

Avg. Late L_t Planned L_t	% Expected Stockouts						
	1.0	*2.5*	*5.0*	*10.0*	*20.0*	*30–59*	*60–100**
1.1	0.0051	0.0026	0.0053	0.0062	0.0069	0.0072	0.0075
1.2	0.0020	0.0051	0.0102	0.0120	0.0133	0.0139	0.0145
1.3	0.0030	0.0075	0.0149	0.0177	0.0196	0.0204	0.0213
1.4	0.0039	0.0098	0.0195	0.0232	0.0257	0.0268	0.0279
1.5	0.0048	0.0119	0.0238	0.0282	0.0313	0.0326	0.0340
1.6	0.0056	0.0140	0.0280	0.0332	0.0368	0.0384	0.0400
1.7	0.0064	0.0160	0.0320	0.0379	0.0420	0.0439	0.0457
1.8	0.0072	0.0181	0.0361	0.0428	0.0475	0.0495	0.0516
1.9	0.0080	0.0200	0.0400	0.0474	0.0525	0.0548	0.2571
2.0	0.0087	0.0218	0.1435	0.2516	0.2572	0.2597	0.2622

*Values from Table 8 @ 15 percent holding cost

Therefore, theoretically, the prevention cost would be independent of the percentage of times an overdue occurs.

However, in practical operation and as would be demonstrated by going through the more complex mathematics of both a leadtime and demand-probability analysis, there will be a lesser reaction and consequently lesser quantity stocked as the certainty of a stock-out decreases. To approximate this reaction, an expected value concept was applied.

This concept involved multiplying the 100 percent column by an approximation of the expected-inventory analyst's reaction to extended delivery. This expected-value approximation shown in the table is not directly applicable to inventory operation but should provide a representative prevention cost for purchasing analysis.

To apply Table 10:

1. Identify the $\dfrac{\text{average late leadtime}}{\text{planned leadtime}}$ factor and find in column 1.
2. Identify the relation of D_{LT}/ORP.
3. Identify the percentage of demand jeopardized from Table 9 using answers 1 and 2 above.
4. Identify "expected stock-outs" by multiplying the percentage of orders late by answer 3 above.
5. Identify the late-delivery valuation factor from Table 10 using answers 1 and 4 above.
6. Multiply answer 5 by the existing safety-stock level to identify the prevention cost.

These steps appear fairly detailed. However, if you have already identified the expected stock-out level to assist in prioritizing expediting, the only additional steps requiring application are steps 5 and 6.

For an example of the complete application, if we assume that the following characteristics apply to the commodity grouping under review,

1. $D_{LT}/ORP = .60$
2. $\dfrac{\text{Average Late Leadtime}}{\text{Standard Leadtime}} = \dfrac{14 \text{ weeks}}{10 \text{ weeks}} = 1.4$
3. Percentage of orders late = 5%
4. Safety stock level of $2,000

application would proceed as follows:

Step Number	Step Description	Answer
1	$\dfrac{\text{Average Late Leadtime}}{\text{Standard Leadtime}} = \dfrac{L_{LT}}{S_{LT}}$	1.4
2	D_{LT}/ORP	.60
3	Percent of demands jeopardized: Answer Table 9 row 4 $(.60 = D_{LT})$ Column 4 $\left(1.4 = \dfrac{L_{LT}}{S_{LT}}\right)$	24.0%
4	"Expected stock-outs" = Percent orders (5%)	1.2%
5	Late delivery valuation factor: answer from Table 10 row 4 $\left(1.4\dfrac{L_{LT}}{S_{LT}}\right)$, column 1 (1.0 closest to 1.2%) (answer 4)	.0039
6	Late-delivery cost: answer 5 (.0039) times safety-stock level ($2,000)	$7.80

With this identification in conjunction with the leadtime-cost valuation method that was discussed, you are in a position to complete a total vendor net-cost analysis. By including the annual dollar value for the leadtime and the unreliable-delivery cost derived above in your hidden-cost ratio, the net-cost formula of NET COST = Price – (Price) (NT) + Price (Hidden-cost ratio) will provide you the total vendor-cost guidance that you require and the separate handling of delivery and hidden-cost factors referenced in Chapter 2 will be unnecessary.

ATTACHMENT 1
LEADTIME–INVENTORY-COST INFLUENCES

Although the leadtime used to calculate ORP affects both the demand during leadtime and the safety-stock calculation, it is only the safety-stock increase that results in increasing inventory costs.

This can be illustrated through the use of the ORP formula and with the inventory diagram that follows. Let us assume that the ORP formula $ORP = D_{LT} + SS_{LT}$ results in a calculated order-review point of ORP_1. In usual application this will mean that an order will be issued to replenish your stock levels when the quantity of material on hand (already in inventory) plus that already on order is less than ORP_1. The actual quantity to be ordered, however, is determined not by the ORP but by an economic-ordering quantity calculation. Thus, the ORP identifies the timing of a replenishment order and an EOQ the quantity. Consequent-

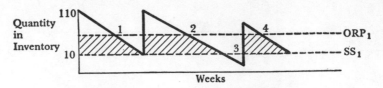

FIGURE 20.   ORP-Demand Influence

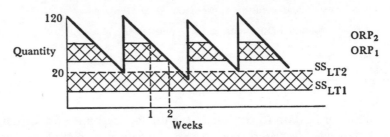

FIGURE 21.   ORP Demand Influence

ly. as illustrated by Figure 20, in which D_{LT} portion of the ORP is represented by the cross-hatched area and SS by the area below, the order-review point value of ORP_1 will trigger a replenishment order at points 1, 2, and 4 for an EOQ quantity of 100, since on hand plus on order is less than ORP and the actual inventory quantity on hand is equal to the remaining EOQ quantity plus the safety stock at any point in the above diagram. At point 3 on the above diagram, the safety-stock levels have been reduced from SS_1. However, in accordance with probability theory, this will rarely happen and the effective safety-stock level can be approximated as SS_1.

If leadtime increases, both components of the ORP, D_{LT} and SS will also increase, since both are functions of leadtime. For the purpose of illustration, let us assume that they increase to provide $ORP_2 = D_{LT2} + SS_2$. The resultant inventory compared to ORP_1 could be illustrated as in Figure 21.

The increase in the D_{LT} portion of the order-review point simply results in an earlier order (compare point 1, D_{LT2} to point 2, D_{LT1}), not an increase in inventory. The SS increase, however, since it is not a regularly used portion of inventory and is independent of the EOQ, not only contributes to an earlier order but also raises inventory levels by $SS_{LT2} - SS_{LT1}$ (cross-hatched area).

ATTACHMENT 2

PERCENTAGE OF DEMAND JEOPARDIZED BY UNPLANNED LATE DELIVERY

As every purchasing man who has expedited orders realizes, there will be instances in which even though a vendor's promise date is missed the overdue has not created a stock-out. This type of situation will occur even in the tightest inventory systems due to the statistical nature of the *ORP* calculation in an uncertain-demand situation.

General Theory

Assuming that your potential demand during leadtime can be illustrated by the normal distribution in Figure 22, in order to provide protection against an unplanned increase in leadtime, this curve must be shifted to the right to provide a larger replenishment stock to cover demands during the extended leadtime.

The *ORP* by definition of the formula must increase in both D_{LT} and safety stock as a result of an increase in leadtime. However, it is still possible to cover a proportion of the potential extended-leadtime demands with the original ORP_1. This occurrence is illustrated by the shaded area above where ORP_1 overlaps the extended-leadtime distribution. Consequently, if the demand during leadtime happened to be low enough (below ORP_1) an overdue replenishment order would not result in an out-of-stock.

The degree of this overlap may be identified by analyzing the characteristics of the unplanned leadtime extension compared to the *ORP* characteristics of D_{LT} and *SS*. Once the overlap is identified, the jeopardized or nonoverlapping demands can also be expressed. This jeopardized demand was expressed in Table 9.

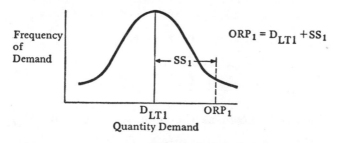

FIGURE 22.

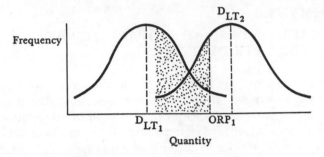

FIGURE 23.   Effect of Leadtime Shift on ORP

Necessary ORP Increase

The first step necessary in the derivation of Table 9 was to determine how much larger the *ORP* would have to be in order to cover all demands possible under selected leadtime extensions. This was done by substituting the matrix numbers from Table 9 into the *ORP* formula of:

$$ORP = (D)(LT) + (SS)(\sqrt{LT})$$

Where: D = Average demand per month
LT = Leadtime in months
SS = Safety stock in months

With this relationship, if the average late delivery was 1.1 times the planned leadtime, the increase in D (LT) would be:

$$D (LT) = 1.1$$

and the increase in SS $(\sqrt{LT})$:

$$SS (\sqrt{LT}) = \sqrt{1.1}$$

The D_{LT}/ORP relationship was then applied to weight the change in each part of the above equation to identify the *ORP*. If we assume that D_{LT} was 90 percent of *ORP*, this would be done as follows:

$$ORP = (.9)\ 1.1 + (.1)\ (\sqrt{1.1})$$

and the net change in *ORP* would be:

$$ORP = .9\ (1.1) + .1\ (\sqrt{1.1}) = 1.095$$

which is the value shown at the intersection of row .9 $\frac{(DLT)}{ORP}$ and column 1.1 $\frac{\text{(average late leadtime)}}{\text{planned leadtime}}$ in the matrix in Table 11.

TABLE 11.   Necessary Increase In ORP To Cover Demands of Indicated Average Late Delivery

*Y	*X						
	1.1	1.2	1.3	1.4	1.5	2.0	3.0
0.9	1.095	1.190	1.280	1.379	1.473	1.952	2.870
0.8	1.090	1.179	1.268	1.357	1.445	1.883	2.747
0.7	1.085	1.169	1.252	1.336	1.418	1.825	2.620
0.6	1.080	1.158	1.236	1.314	1.390	1.766	2.493
0.5	1.075	1.148	1.220	1.293	1.363	1.708	2.367
0.4	1.070	1.138	1.204	1.271	1.335	1.649	2.240
0.3	1.065	1.127	1.188	1.250	1.308	1.591	2.113
0.2	1.060	1.117	1.172	1.228	1.280	1.532	1.986
0.1	1.055	1.107	1.156	1.207	1.256	1.423	1.860

*Definition of X and Y

$$X = \frac{\text{Average Late Leadtime}}{\text{Planned Leadtime}}$$

$$Y = \frac{D_{LT}}{ORP}$$

In summary, the equation applied to identify the necessary ORP change was:

Equation 13

$$\Delta ORP = Y(X) + (1-Y)(\sqrt{X})$$

Where: $Y = D_{LT}/ORP$

$$X = \frac{\text{Average Late Leadtime}}{\text{Planned Leadtime}}$$

Estimation of Resulting Stock-outs

With identification of the ORP, it was then possible to approximate the necessary shift of the curve to protect all demands, and translate this shift to the probability of the demand coverage of the original ORP relative to the ORP requirement necessary with each average late delivery, D_{LT}/ORP combination in Table 9.

This was done by using the following formulation to explain the shift in terms of standard deviations:

Equation 14

$$\text{Standard Deviation} = \frac{(1.0 - ((Y)\,(X)))}{(Y\,(X)) - (\Delta ORP)}(1.645)$$

The constant in this term (1.645) assumes the use of a 95 percent one-tail confidence factor.

To convert the standard deviations to probabilities and identify the jeopardized demand, the following steps were taken for each matrix block in Table 9.

1. If the result was negative,
    a. Convert the resulting number of standard deviations to probabilities with the use of a normal-distribution table.
    b. Add 45 percent.
2. If the result was positive,
    a. Convert the resulting number of standard deviations to probabilities with the use of a normal-distribution table.
    b. Subtract from 45 percent to find the applicable matrix percentage.

Example
$$Y = \ .0$$
$$X = 1.1$$
$$ORP = \ .095 \text{ (from table)}$$

Apply Formula
$$\text{Std. deviations} = \frac{(1.0 - (.9)(1.1))}{(1.1)\,(.9) - (.095))} \times (1.645)$$
$$= .173$$

Convert to Probability
$$173 \text{ standard deviation} = .067$$

Positive $\therefore$ *subtract from 45%*
$$45.0 - 6.7 = 38.3\% \text{ (answer in table)}$$

ATTACHMENT 3

EXPECTED STOCK-OUT-PREVENTION COST

Table 8 provides cost multipliers for necessary safety-stock additions with respect to leadtime changes. These additions will provide the same proportionate demand protection expected with the original *ORP*.

In the case of stock-out prevention, as was seen from Table 9, not all unplanned overdues or leadtime extensions will result in stock-outs and consequently not all will require the full safety-stock adjustments displayed in Table 9.

The theoretically correct method of identifying this interplay and approximating the necessary safety-stock increases would be to compute a leadtime distribution as well as a demand distribution and identify an *ORP* common to both. However, with respect to the potential gain in information compared to the expense required to compensate for increasing computational complexity, it is felt that the technique below offers a greater value.

Derivation of Weighting Factors

This technique involves a pragmatic approach to anticipating an inventory analyst's reaction in terms of safety-stock additions to estimated levels of out-of-stock demands. The reaction model in this application takes the form of a standard inventory concept, the "ABC" or "Pareto" curve, shown in Figure 24.

The observation expressed by this curve is that a small number of orders, accounts, etc., will represent a high proportion of the total inventory value. Although this curve is not usually used to represent human reaction, it seems to fit the response situation under discussion.

For instance, if an inventory analyst identifies an out-of-stock situation but recognizes that it happens only 1 out of 100 times (1.0 percent), his reaction would be expected to be very minor. In accordance with the above curve, he would attempt to adjust the inventory by increasing safety stock to 14 percent of the full extended-leadtime safety stock. If,

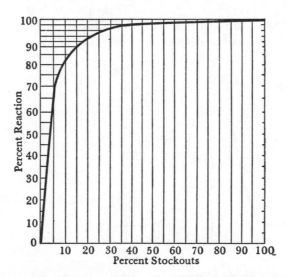

FIGURE 24. Safety Stock Reaction to Leadtime Extension

however, he reaches an unplanned out-of-stock condition of 5 percent of the orders, his reaction will be much more severe (70 percent). This, again, could be expected. If, as in most inventory systems, the analyst is using a 95 percent coverage factor in his *ORP* calculations, this 5 percent stock-out level has in effect doubled his desired number of stock-outs. Yet, one would not expect his reaction to be so severe that he stocks the full extended-leadtime safety stock for 5 to 100 cases. At 20 percent stock-outs the account would be so unreliable and the manufacturing pressure so great due to stock-outs that one would expect nearly a full reaction as illustrated by the curve's (92 percent).

Besides seeming to approximate inventory reactions, it is felt that the curve should also provide results close to those available through working with both a demand and leadtime distribution.

Take the curve illustration of the 70 percent adjustment for the 5 percent stock-out level (Figure 25). If we assume that the leadtime extension jeopardized 100 percent of the possible demands, the vendor-overdue factor must be 5 percent since stock-outs will equal jeopardized demands times the percentage of vendor overdues.

With the analyst's 70 percent reaction, he would be able to cover all but 8 percent of the possible demands (.7 × 1.645 standard deviations converted to probability). Which gives an adjusted anticipated stock-out level of only .4 percent (5 percent times 8 percent) which is only 8 percent in excess of desired levels.

Generation of Table 10

In applying this curve to generate Table 10, the full *SS* for the referenced leadtime extension (100 percent column) was multiplied by the percentage in the curve displayed previously to identify the expected coverage cost.

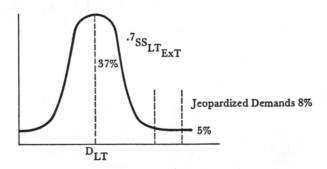

FIGURE 25. Illustration of Safety Stock Adjustment

$\equiv$Appendix 6

ESCALATION HEDGE: QUANTITY BREAK

This appendix reviews not only the derivation of the tables referenced in conjunction with the escalation-hedge and quality-break procedures but also identifies the costs applicable to each decision and how to easily modify these tables for your identified costs.

EFFECTIVE COST-IDENTIFICATION

Aside from simplifying these decision processes as was done by the procedures in the third chapter, the critical element in effective extended procurement and in making these procedures applicable to you is identification of the applicable costs of these activities. Both quantity buying and escalation hedging require an investment in inventories. Consequently, both require identification of the actual cost to carry inventory and the necessary return required to invest funds in this manner in order to assure that the lowest-cost decision can be reached. Failure to properly determine these costs has led to much of the unsatisfactory experience associated with quantity-buying and hedging.

Return on Investment

Just as you would not put your funds in a savings account without an adequate return, you should not request an investment in hedging or quantity-buy inventories without a savings sufficient to justify the investment. In reviewing the fund requirements associated with these decisions on a commodity-by-commodity basis, it would be easy to draw the conclusion that the effective necessary return on investments is so low that it should be ignored since each individual investment is short-lived and fairly small.

However, when hedging or quantity-buying occurs across all your commodities, as will happen when you initiate a full-scale extended procurement program, these decisions reoccur and overlap becoming continual, significant fund absorbers. Applications in steel and finished material procurement for heavy manufacturing have resulted in a 20-30 percent inventory increase compared to procuring *EOQ* quantities. Therefore, you are actually competing for funds with capital investments and other asset accounts when you make hedge and quantity-buy decisions since you are restricting fund availability.

Since many division and company managers are being evaluated on their profit/assets performance, increasing your assets through an increase in inventory without providing an acceptable return on investment will result in a deteriorating performance evaluation. However, including the necessary return on investment in your hedging and quantity-buy decisions will assure not only that you make the correct decision but also further your management's asset-utilization objectives.

Setting this inventory return on investment helps overcome another potential roadblock to effective extended procurement, the establishment of arbitrary inventory objectives. Failure to realize that inventory can serve a profit rather than just a material-availability function leads to setting inviolate, arbitrary objectives for inventory levels (e.g., "We will carry no more than $1 million in inventory") since the cost of material unavailability is difficult to quantify and analyze objectively. Return on investment consideration enables you to demonstrate that this type of investment not only pays for itself in terms of price savings but further contributes to increased material availability and should be undertaken regardless of the existing relationship between on-hand levels and inventory objectives.

Since these decisions produce a relatively low-risk, guaranteed yield investment, your *ROI* should be set at the minimum acceptable pretax return for your total business. This *ROI* will be lower than that required for capital investments since there is less risk, but higher than borrowing costs alone, due to the fact that you cannot avoid the inventory risks associated with your particular business.

Applicable Holding Cost

Identifying the necessary *ROI*, however, will be meaningless unless the inventory-holding cost used to determine it reflects the actual cost that will be incurred. To be effective, these holding costs must be tailored to the commodity and situation at hand. The holding cost can be defined for all inventory-related decisions as the cost incurred in investing money in material that must be stored or held prior to use. This cost is applicable whenever material ordered exceeds the immediately usable requirements whether or not the material is earmarked as a stocked material.

The holding cost is further defined as potentially being composed of the following cost elements: interest charges on money committed to stored material, taxes, insurance, deterioration, obsolescence, labor to hold material (receiving, material control, storekeeper), and value of space taken by inventory. It is computed today, in most companies, by averaging total inventory-related expense in these categories by the total dollar value of inventory on hand.

$$\text{Avg. Holding Cost} = \frac{\text{Total inventory related expense}}{\text{Total value of inventory}}$$

However, certain publications have rightly suggested that total expense is not an adequate portrayal. They indicate that the only costs applicable to these types of decisions are those variable portions (costs that increase or decrease directly with the value of inventory) since it is only these costs that decrease the price advantage available in hedging or quantity-break buying. Those costs (fixed) that do not increase as inventory levels rise will be incurred regardless of the on-hand inventory and, thus, cannot be an acceptable portion of the decision-making criteria.

As an illustration of this thought, when a purchasing decision involves increasing the quantity of material ordered but does not require creating a new inventory account, charges for space and labor are not applicable until you reach a certain critical limit. If one additional plate or valve is added to normal requirements, it would be rare that an extra pile or bin would be required or that extra people would have to be hired to handle the material. In fact, as the quantity-per-order is raised, there will be fewer ordering situations per year indicating that there would even be a reduction in inventory-associated labor, and since these increases would be temporary, existing space, if available, would in all likelihood be better used.

The variable-cost concept takes a large step towards providing an actual cost of holding inventory, but unless this concept is applied to specific commodities rather than averaging the usually variable costs across all commodities, it can also lead to poor decisions. Deterioration, for instance, appears to be an obvious variable cost of holding inventory since, as more is stocked of a given material, more money will be expected to be lost through deterioration. Yet, when deterioration is averaged across different commodity groups such as nickel materials and photoelectric cells and applied to each in determining how much to buy, you will buy too little nickel and too many photoelectric cells, losing on both counts since nickel deterioration is insignificant compared to that of the cells.

Identifying average cost by individual commodity grouping, however, is not only extremely costly but close to impossible. This is due to the necessity of investigating all differing commodity groups for different quantities and group-ordering mixes in order to effectively identify significant costs.

As a practical compromise, it would seem beneficial to initiate the decision using only the minimum costs that are variable in accordance with the inventoried value for all commodities and then to review on an as-required basis the necessity of considering the other costs. For instance, the space consideration is indeed important; but the critical question with respect to hedging and quantity-breaks is, "Do I have it or don't I?", not "What does it cost?" If space is available, it is simply better to use space by filling it with this type of material. Does it make any sense to cultivate dead space and let savings possibilities escape by restricting the quantity procured through application of average-space cost if space is available? Consequently, first find out if extended procurement presents opportunities with respect to the other costs. Then, review the available space.

A similar approach must be applied with respect to deterioration and obsolescence. You certainly do not want to hedge three months of material if the shelf life is two months. (An average-cost figure will not tell this.) But for most of your commodities, without going through a detailed analysis, it is easy to determine that shelf life is at least a year or greater and the resulting deterioration and obsolescence is insignificant. Therefore, it makes little sense to restrict your hedge or quantity-buying in these long-life commodities to guard against shorter shelf life in other commodities.

If you start with the costs that are variable for all commodities with respect to inventory value, return on investment, and insurance and taxes, and review the other potential costs on a "go or no go" basis as instructed by the procedures in the third chapter you will be in a position to optimize your decision because the cost will fit the situation and characteristics of the commodity under investigation.

Purchase Order Processing Cost

There is also an additional cost that must be considered with respect to those decisions that relate to purchase order processing. The effect of this cost is reviewed below from both the escalation-hedge and quantity-break perspectives.

Escalation Hedge

In establishing a hedge-buy system it is necessary to identify, as was done in the inventory-cost analysis, which potential costs or savings will actually affect your total costs. Although it would appear that, since you are buying more per order, hedging would produce savings, it is necessary to look a little further to see if this paper reduction is significant enough to result in an actual savings. In this review, two factors are of consequence: first, hedging does not occur at regular intervals for each buyer throughout the year but only when increases in his commodity occur. Thus, resulting paper reductions are sporadic. Second, many hedge applications do not result in combining orders but simply issuing the same number of orders earlier or with earlier required dates.

The key to obtaining a cost savings from a paperwork reduction is capitalizing on this reduction through reduced staffing or greater cost improvement. But, since hedging is sporadic, there is no opportunity for a reduction in clerical personnel. If you attempt to decrease your clerical force in reaction to a hedging paperwork reduction, you will be faced with the inefficiency of having to rehire laid-off personnel since the work load will quickly rise again. Further, there is little opportunity for a buyer to improve his cost-reduction yield since it is unlikely that he will be able to adjust his work patterns to the reduced ordering load quickly enough to substantially improve his performance.

Aside from the above considerations, a paperwork-load reduction may never be realized since many hedges will result in the issuance of nearly the same amount of paper as if the hedging activity had not been initiated. This is due to the increasing desirability of identifying purchased material with respect to production contracts. In many instances when hedge requests are initiated, your order-writers will simply issue the same number of orders with specific contract identification, but will issue them earlier or with earlier required dates. In this way they are able to keep track of material and contract receipts while also achieving the hedging advantages.

Since it is doubtful that either a significant paper reduction or one that can be turned to your cost advantage can be achieved through hedging, the hedge system has ignored this as a potential savings in its decision technique.

Quantity-Break

Unlike the hedge application, quantity-break decisions will recur throughout the year and will significantly reduce the paperwork flow. Simulations have shown that quantity-break buying compared to *EOQ-*

buying for steel and finished goods is capable of increasing order quantities by approximately 20 percent which results in 20 percent purchase-order-processing load reduction. Since this load reduction is continuous and significant, it provides the opportunity to reduce clerical staffing and/or apply greater effort towards improvement of performance. Consequently, the quantity-break techniques include consideration of purchase-order-processing savings as well as the necessary return on investment and holding cost.

DERIVATION OF TABLES

In order to derive the Escalation Hedge, Quantity Break, and Order Savings Tables referred to in Chapter 3, it was necessary to formulate the relation between *ROI*, price advantage, inventory holding cost, and quantity of additional material procured, as well as the net savings or cost, which is the price advantage minus the effective inventory holding cost.

Escalation Hedge Tables

In order to compute columns 1 and 2 in the hedge table, it was necessary to identify a formula for the number of months of excess material that should be procured at an anticipated price advantage in order to provide a sufficient return on investment (*ROI*) to justify the investment.

Since it is commonly accepted in financial theory that incremental investments should be cut off when the yield is equal to or lower than the prespecified *ROI*, it is necessary to identify that month at which the price advantage minus the inventory holding cost equals the necessary *ROI*.

This equality is depicted in the following formula:

Equation 15

$$\%ROI = \left((\%P) \times \frac{(12)}{N}\right) - \%h$$

where: $\%P$ = Percentage price advantage =
$$\frac{P_2 - P_1}{P_1}(100)$$

P_1 = Price before increase
P_2 = New price after escalation
N = Number of months usage represented by hedge quantity
$\%h$ = Applicable inventory carrying cost per annum less the cost of money in a percentage

$$\%ROI = \text{Required return on investment per}$$
$$\text{annum in a percentage}$$

The $\frac{(12)}{N}$ factor in the above equation was used to convert the price advantage for material procured to an annual figure enabling creation of the equality with the annual ROI and h.

h is defined as the applicable inventory holding cost per annum less the cost of money. It is necessary to extract the cost of money from the inventory carrying charge for this comparison since financial analysis dictates that investment comparisons assume the availability of money and must be made irrespective of financing alternatives.

Column 1 in the hedge table was derived by solving Equation 15 for P (price increase) sequentially for each of the hedge figures referred to in column 2. This process may be illustrated as follows:

$$\text{Since } \%ROI = \left((\%P) \times \frac{(12)}{N}\right) - \%h,$$

$$\%P = \frac{(\%ROI + \%h)\ N}{12}$$

Therefore, in solving for $\%P$, to identify the necessary price increase when $N = 1$ (first row, column 2 in table) and given the values for $\%h$ (7%) and $\%ROI$ (15%), we obtain:

$$\%P_1 = \frac{(15 + 7)1}{12} = 1.8\%$$

which is the same answer as in row 1, column 1 for $\%P$.

This process was then repeated for $N = 2, 3, 4 \ldots 12$ to complete the rest of the values in the $\%P$ column.

Identifying the savings resulting from each decision (column 3) necessitated expressing the total applicable holding cost rather than the highest incremental cost as was done in Equation 15.

To identify this total holding cost, it was necessary to relate the applicable holding cost to the amount of material hedged and the amount of time that incremental amounts would remain in inventory. The following equation expresses this relationship.

Equation 16

$$h_{mt} = \sum_{x=1}^{x=n} \frac{h_m}{365} (S_x)(P_1)\, x$$

Where: h_{mt} = Total variable carrying cost including cost of money

n = Total days required to use hedged quantity of material

h_m = Decimal annual, total, variable holding cost including cost of money

S_x = Quantity that will be used each of the respective (n) days

x = Hedge supply day 1, 2, 3 ... n

P_1 = Current price per unit

It was then necessary to formulate the expected dollar savings in order to proceed towards identification of the percentage expected savings.

Equation 17 below expresses the dollar savings available from any given hedge decision.

Equation 17

$$\text{Dollar Savings} = ((P_2 - P_1)(S_t)) - h_{mt}$$

Where: P_2 = Anticipated escalated price

P_1 = Current price

S_t = Total number of units hedged

h_{mt} = Total variable carrying cost including cost of money

In order to convert this dollar savings to the percentage expected savings, Equation 17 must be divided by the value of material hedged (P_1) (S_t) and multiplied by 100. The result of these adjustments is expressed below.

Equation 18

$$\% \text{ Savings} = \%P - \%h_{mt}$$

Where: $\%P$ = Percentage price advantage =

$$\frac{P_2 - P_1}{P_1}(100)$$

$\%h_{mt}$ = Percentage holding cost =

$$\sum_{x=1}^{x=n} \frac{h_m(S_x) \times (100)}{365 \, (S_t)}$$

This formula was simplified through the assumption of consistent monthly demand in order to enable computation without knowing the specific demand for each hedge day as required by Equation 18. The simplified result below was the equation used to compute column 3 in the hedge table.

Equation 19

$$\text{Estimated Savings} = \left(\%P - \frac{\%h_m}{12} \ (X_{me}) \right)$$

Where: $\%P$ = Percentage price advantage
$\%h_m$ = Percentage annual holding cost
X_{me} = Median month hedged

To illustrate how this formula was applied in development of column 3, refer to row 3 of the escalation hedge table. In this row $\%P$ (first column) is equal to 5.5%, the hedge in months is 3 and, for this table, the $\%h_m$ used was 15%. Thus, X_{me} (median month hedged) is equal to 2 and

$$\text{Estimated \% Savings} = 5.5 - \left(\frac{15}{12} \times 2 \right) = 3.0\%$$

which is the same answer as that recorded in row 3, column 3 of the hedge table.

Quantity-Break Table

The price-quantity-break decision requires identifying the minimum price and purchase-order-processing savings that must be obtained in order to equal the holding cost resulting from early procurement of the price-break quantity minus the normal ordering quantity and the *ROI* required in order to justify this advance procurement. This relationship can be expressed as follows:

Equation 20

$$\%P + \%O \geqslant \%Y$$

Where: $\%P$ = Percentage price advantage
$$\frac{P_2 - P_1}{P_1}(100)$$
and
P_1 = Price-break price
P_2 = Original quantity price
$\%O$ = Percentage order-cost savings $\dfrac{O_d}{P_1 S_t}$ (100)
and
O_d = Order-cost savings in dollars
S_t = Price-break quantity in units
$\%Y$ = Minimum acceptable yield required to engage in quantity-buy (in a percentage)

$$\sum_{x=1}^{x=n} (ROI + h) \left(\frac{x}{365}\right) S_x P_1 (100)$$

and

ROI = Decimal, annual necessary return on investment

h = Decimal, annual holding cost less the cost of money

n = Total days excess supply = days required to use quantity-break quantity minus days required to use original order quantity

x = Excess supply day 1, 2, 3 . . . n

S_x = Quantity that will be used in each respective excess supply day.

The quantity-break procedure directs you to investigate the savings–minimum acceptable yield balance associated with this formula. The table generation, however, required solution of this equation for %Y in order to facilitate this investigation. In order to simplify this computation, the results of Equation 20 were approximated with the assumption of consistent demand as follows:

Equation 21

$$\%Y = (\%h + \%ROI)\frac{X_e}{12} \left(\frac{1}{2}\right)$$

Where: %h = Percentage applicable annual holding cost (no cost of money should be included).

%ROI = Necessary annual percentage return on investment required.

X_e = Total excess months supply represented price-break minus original quantity.

In this equation (%h + %ROI) represents the combined annual return that must be obtained to justify procuring an excess quantity that will be held for a full year without use. The factor $\frac{X_e}{12}$ adjusts the return from an annual figure to the return required for the actual number of months that the excess will be outstanding. ½ further adjusts the necessary return to account for the fact that, assuming consistent demand, material will be used regularly throughout the investment period. Consequently, the effective investment is only half of the ordered excess and requires this adjustment to accurately depict the outstanding investment.

This equation was applied to determine the necessary values in column 2 by sequentially introducing the values for X_e in column 1 into the above formula. To illustrate this process, let us review the calculation of the %Y (minimum acceptable yield) in row 6 of the quantity-break table. Since a %ROI of 15% and a %h of 7% was assumed in the creation of this table and row 6 contains an X_e value of 6 in column 1, the %Y for row 6, column 2 is calculated as follows:

$$\%Y6 = (7\% + 15\%)\left(\frac{6}{12}\right)\left(\frac{1}{2}\right) = 5.5\%$$

which is the same answer contained in column 2 of row 6.

The percentage inventory cost (column 3) was obtained in a similar manner through a derivative of Equation 21:

Equation 22

$$\% \text{ Cost} = h_m \frac{(X_e)}{24}$$

Where: h_m = Total variable inventory hold cost

Through application of this formula, the cost in the previous example (6 months X_e) at a 15% (h_m) is:

$$\text{Cost} = 15\% \frac{(6)}{24} = 3.8\%$$

which is the answer in the third column of the table for row 6.

Purchase Order Savings

In identifying the purchase-order-processing cost savings resulting from procuring extended quantities, it was necessary to first find the number of orders saved by buying in quantity-break rather than normal quantity lots and then to multiply this answer, minus 1, by the purchase-order-processing cost, to find the net savings. This is done in the following formula which was applied to derive the purchase order savings table.

Equation 23

$$O_d = \left(\frac{(X_t)}{(X_t - X_e)} - 1\right)(PO_c)$$

Where: O_d = Net purchase-order-processing cost
savings
X_t = Number of months supply represented
by price-break quantity

$$X_e = \text{Excess months supply in price-break}$$
$$\text{quantity}$$
$$PO_c = \text{Purchase-order-processing cost per order}$$

The dollar savings figures in the table were derived by assuming a $13/order processing cost and solving for the values of X_t and X_e indicated by the respective columns and rows of the table.

TABLE MODIFICATION INSTRUCTIONS

As was pointed out in the introduction, one of the factors prohibiting widespread use of existing tabled techniques is a lack of a simple modification device for alternate costs to those used in the example tables. The procedures below have been provided to solve this problem. They will enable you to modify the hedge and quantity-break tables for your applicable minimal acceptable return, processing cost, and inventory holding cost, with just simple multiplication.

Escalation Hedge Table — Modification Procedure

In making this modification, the first step must be to identify your actual costs.

1. Identification of your costs
   a. Insurance
      Divide annual inventory insurance premium by maximum value of inventory insurance coverage
   b. Taxes
      Divide inventory taxes by the inventory tax valuation
   c. Other costs
      Identify percentage value of inventory for any other costs which you would prefer to include as minimum tabled cost (perhaps deterioration or obsolescence)
   d. Identify your necessary return on investment (ROI)
   e. Identify your minimal acceptable return
      Add the results from a, b, c, and d to find the applicable percentage inventory insurance, taxes, and other costs
2. Column 1 modification
   Multiply each figure in column 1 in the escalation hedge table by the following ratio:
   $$\frac{\text{Your minimal acceptable return}}{22\%} \text{ (identified above)}$$
3. Column 3 modification

a. Add your percentage borrowing cost to a, b, and c above to determine your percentage inventory cost for this decision
b. Multiply each figure in column 3 by the following ratio:

$$\frac{\text{Your percentage inventory cost}}{15\%}$$

to convert column 3 numbers to those applicable to your costs.

Once you have applied these modification directions to the escalation hedge table, you will have converted the hedge procedure to one that can be efficient and effective in producing hedging-cost savings for your company. The quantity-break procedure that follows is very similar in scope but does have some basic differences.

Quantity-Break — Modification Procedure

The quantity-break table may be modified by the following procedure:

I. Quantity-break table modification
   A. Divide annual inventory insurance premium by maximum value of inventory insurance coverage
   B. Divide inventory taxes by the inventory tax valuation
   C. Add the result from A and B to find percentage inventory insurance and taxes
   D. Column 2 modification
      1. Add your *ROI* to percentage inventory insurance and taxes to determine minimal acceptable return for this decision
      2. To convert column 2 for your costs, multiply each figure in column 2 by the ratio

$$\frac{\text{Your minimal acceptable return}}{22\%}$$

   E. Column 3 modification
      1. Add cost of borrowing to division percentage inventory insurance and taxes to determine percentage inventory cost for this decision
      2. To convert column 3 for your costs, multiply each figure in column 3 by the ratio

$$\frac{\text{Your percentage inventory cost}}{15\%}$$

    II. Purchase-order-savings table modification
        A. Identify purchase-order-processing cost by instructions in Appendix 7
        B. Multiply each number in this table by the following ratio in order to convert this table for your costs

$$\frac{\text{Your processing cost}}{\$13}$$

Through application of this modification technique, you will have created a quantity-break procedure that presents an easy application, effectively represents your costs, and will meet your return-on-investment objectives in decisionmaking. In both of these decision areas, application of this procedure will substantially increase your buyers' yields and allow them to use two of the more sophisticated procurement tools available with a minimum of effort and training.

$\overline{\underline{\;}}$Appendix 7

CLERICAL COST PER DOCUMENT

There are three basic methods currently in use that are available to value the clerical load associated with purchasing: accounting, opportunity cost, and time estimate.

The accounting method is the most traditionally applied. This method, in most cases, ignores all but purchase-order costs and computes the cost to process a purchase order as follows:

$$\text{P.O. Cost} = \frac{\text{Total Ordering-Related Expense}}{\text{\#Purchase Orders Issued}}$$

This method, besides offering no opportunity for valuing clerical activities other than issuing purchase orders, has one major flaw. It assumes that the only activities of a purchasing department are paper processing. It completely ignores the fact that these clerical activities only help keep purchasing's head above water, while it is the improvement activities that make purchasing most valuable.

Since this method turns its back on purchasing's cost-improvement function, serious order-processing cost distortions can result. As an illustration of such a distortion, consider the situation in which the number of orders issued decreases. Since purchasing has a cost-improvement, as well as a clerical function, the purchasing budget will not be directly responsive to clerical-load changes. Therefore, as the number of orders drops, the cost to issue a purchase order in using this computation method will increase, even though it takes no more time or expense to physically handle a purchase order with the decreased load than before the load reduction. The response to this processing-cost increase will be higher order quantities, as a result of *EOQ* calculations that use this cost, and a consequent increase in inventory cost which cannot be justified by actual ordering-cost tradeoffs. In this manner, this cost depiction can lead you astray from cost-minimizing decisions.

The opportunity-cost method overcomes this problem but is the least commonly used of any of the three, due to the difficulty associated with its valuation. This method makes an assumption, directly opposed to the accounting approximation, that there is greater value in purchasing's improvement activities than in purchasing's clerical duties. Consequently, the clerical time is valued by relating purchasing clerical time expended to opportunities lost for cost improvements.

Theoretically, this relation can be developed by comparing clerical load over a period of time to cost-improvement performance, as in Figure 26.

In this diagram, cost-improvement performance is related to a relative measure (time units) of time expended to issue clerical documents. Time units must be used rather than numbers of documents in order to provide a measure that is consistent from year to year, for an accurate relationship between yield and clerical load. To illustrate the need for time units, consider this example. If processing P.O.'s takes twice as long as processing change notices, and change notices rise in proportion to P.O.'s from 1 to 2, a count of clerical documents alone would indicate that paperwork had risen 50 percent, when the time required to process these documents in fact increased only by 25 percent. A measure of documents alone would seriously distort the actual measure of time taken away from improvement activities.

The basic problem with this technique, although it offers the greatest potential in clarifying the role of purchasing and measuring the cost of processing activities, is that this type of improvement-data and time-unit history is not currently collected in most purchasing departments. Thus, a measure and consequent approximation would not be available for a number of years.

The third method, time approximation, appears to offer a suitable interim alternative. As was discussed above, the expression of clerical load in time units is one key element of the opportunity-cost valuation. In the time approximation, these time units, instead of being related to

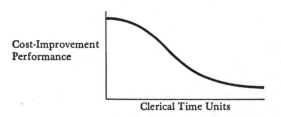

FIGURE 26. Clerical Opportunity Cost

improvement performance, are related to average salary and overhead per hour in order to value clerical cost. This technique, as in the opportunity model, requires an expression of processing time for each type of clerical activity for all interfacing departments. For instance:

$$\text{Purchase order} = 10 \text{ minutes}$$
$$\text{Change notice} = 5 \text{ minutes}$$
$$\text{Proposition} = 15 \text{ minutes}$$
$$\text{Average letter} = 20 \text{ minutes}$$

Once this information is portrayed, it is a simple matter to apply the count of each document and multiply by the hourly rate to determine the clerical-cost contribution for a vendor or commodity.

As an application of this cost-quantification method, the following procedural review for purchase-order processing costs will be of value.

1. Contact material/production control, purchasing, receiving and accounting personnel to obtain an estimate of the average clerical minutes required to physically perform the following activities:

Activity	Dept.
Identify an ordering situation and create a requisition.	Material/Production Control
Make inquiry, select vendor, issue, file a typical order.	Purchasing
Expedite	Material/Production Control Purchasing
Receive material against an order.	Receiving Inspection
Log receipts and pay for material.	Accounts Payable

2. Identify the average total-processing minutes by adding the above estimates.

3. Multiply: $\dfrac{\text{Total time in minutes}}{60} \times$ average hourly salary rate in dollars $\times$ 1.15 to obtain *your processing cost*

Note:

1. Recognizing that each department performs more than just clerical functions, the time required to process will be much less than total time available in each department.

2. Material purchased directly for a contract rather than for stock will require a much greater time than stock material. Therefore, separate estimates should be submitted and utilized.

If the assumption holds that purchasing is expected to perform improvement as well as clerical activities, this measure should provide a good approximation of actual cost expended, since a clerk could be brought in to handle the load or dismissed at the computed cost.

⹀Appendix 8

PURCHASING CLERICAL-COST VALUATION

In order to identify your highest-value processing-cost activities, it is recommended that you follow the steps below. First, however, let us investigate the costs actually affected by clerical load. The costs influenced by purchasing's clerical activities may be grouped into two classifications: inventory and clerical costs.

Besides the actual time consumed in clerical activities and the consequent costs expended, there is the additional cost of inventory that will be incurred in order to minimize the mix of stocking and potential processing costs.

Clerical-*EOQ* Influence

Technically, once a decision has been made to stock a material, an infinite number of orders could be issued for very small quantities at a time to minimize inventory costs. However, in order to avoid excessive clerical costs, an economical order quantity (*EOQ*) is calculated to identify that order quantity that provides the lowest total of order-related inventory and clerical cost. Therefore, the inventory holding cost associated with the *EOQ* is actually the result of the existence of clerical costs. As these costs decrease, the *EOQ* and associated holding costs will also decrease.

Since the full *EOQ* does not remain in inventory year round, but is used to support manufacturing operations, the effective inventory required over time due to clerical costs is the average *EOQ*. Consequently, to value the inventory cost contribution of clerical activities, you may use the following formula:

Equation 24

$$\text{Clerical Inventory Cost} = \tfrac{1}{2}\,EOQ \times h$$

Where: EOQ = the economical ordering quantity in dollars

h^1 = variable holding cost percentage composed of interest, taxes, insurance, deterioration, obsolescence

Again, to minimize data-collection expense, if you request your inventory control group to identify those 10 to 20 commodity groupings that provide the largest EOQ stock requirements and the accompanying stock levels, you can concentrate on those highest-cost contributions and provide this cost approximation at a nominal expense. It is also important in applying this valuation to use only the EOQ dollar value prior to including price breaks in the EOQ calculation, for it is only this value that is influenced by clerical costs.

Purchasing Clerical Cost

The other cost associated with purchasing clerical activities is the actual clerical expense incurred. There are two key pieces of data required to value this activity: Physical count of paper by types of paper handled by commodity/vendor, and identification of the value attached to each type of paper.

The physical count of requisitions, change notices, proposition proposals, etc., offers little problem and is currently collected by most departments since it is valuable as a performance-workload measure for clerical personnel. In order to provide vendor-clerical cost information, all you will do is to slightly modify this counting process. This can be done by putting a check in a buyer-vendor matrix, similar to Form 15, for your major paper-volume vendors as you count the number of documents issued. Once you have completed such a count, you can value these documents as instructed by Appendix 7. You thus will have provided both the inventory and clerical cost associated with purchasing clerical activities.

FORM 15. Clerical-Load Collection Form

Buyer B Vendor	P. Orders	Propositions	Memos	Etc.
X	111			
Y	1		11	
Z		1111		
Etc.				

[1]Note: Space and labor charges should be excluded in this variable holding cost.

$\equiv$Appendix 9

VENDOR QUALIFICATION

One of the initial steps in new source development is discovering if the new vendor is qualified to reliably produce the commodity of interest. This topic is covered in many other books. However, its presentation is most typically couched in a discussion of "vendor ratings," which includes not only initial vendor qualification (survey of the vendor's plant, personnel, financial status, and processing mechanisms), but also vendor-performance evaluation to identify when a reaudit (vendor surveillance) is necessary and for use in selecting vendors. In reality, however, these activities are distinctly separate in approach and application.

1. *Qualification* is the necessary prelude to vendor selection; it identifies a "set" of vendors who are physically qualified to produce the desired commodity.
2. *Vendor selection* involves selecting from this set of vendors the one that offers the greatest value with respect to quoted provisions and cost of performance.
3. *Requalification* is desirable on a routine basis for critical commodities, as determined by your quality department, or only when a vendor's nonperformance is contributing a large portion of your material-related cost due to late delivery or claims, in which case a reaudit must be conducted to identify the direction to take to improve performance (such as process revision, redesign, or alternate vendor).

We have already discussed approaches to vendor selection in Chapter 2, and have also identified the means of spotting candidates for whom a requalification survey would be desirable. Now, let us review the essential ingredients to an efficient vendor-qualification program. As has been stated, qualification requires determining whether a vendor has the physical capability to reliably produce an acceptable product. In order to be qualified, the vendor must have an acceptable financial status, plant layout and necessary equipment, effective processing mechanisms and controls, and qualified and reliable personnel.

One method of determining if a vendor has the necessary capability would be to initiate a vendor-plant audit together with your quality and manufacturing personnel. However, audits are costly and it is possible to simplify an audit and reduce the necessary number of audits required through the use of Form 16 as you make inquiries to new sources.

Once the information on this form is returned with the bid, you will have the necessary information to determine if a physical audit of the vendor plant appears desirable. If a vendor who has not been previously qualified submits the most attractive bid, proceed as follows with the qualification information to determine if an audit is desirable:

1. *Is this vendor's financial standing acceptable?*
    a. Is this vendor's debt/equity ratio equal or below other vendors in this same industry?
    b. Is this vendor's short-term assets (cash, receivables, government securities) short term liability equal or above that of other vendors in this same industry?
    c. Does the volume represented by the commodity under review represent a small portion of this vendor's total sales value?
    d. Will management plan reverse favorable position of any of the above findings?
    e. If these questions can all be answered with "yes," barring extreme situations, this vendor presents a sound financial position. If answers to some of the above questions are "no," discuss these outcomes further with the vendor to identify the cause for the ratios being lower than the industry and to determine if this situation is critical to your procurement.
2. *Is the plant adequate?* Review facility list, planned expansion or changes, layout, and flow with Quality and Manufacturing to determine if the results are adequate.
3. *Personnel*
    a. Review labor history to determine labor-force reliability.
    b. Review and note key personnel and back-ups to identify:
        1) Contacts.
        2) Likelihood of continuation of effective operation.
        3) Personnel to interview in the event of a plant audit.
4. *Quality and testing certifications.* Review certifications with your quality personnel to assure vendor's credentials are adequate for production of this commodity.

FORM 16. Vendor-Qualification Form

Information Required	Form in Which Required
I. Financial	1. Provide current Dun and Bradstreet Analytical Report and/or current annual report or comparable financial-status information. 2. Provide annual report or comparable financial information for last three years. 3. Describe planned changes significantly affecting the above status.
II. Plant	1. Provide current name and location of plant for referenced commodity. 2. Provide facility list. 3. Describe planned expansions or changes. 4. Provide schematic of plant layout. 5. Describe flow through plant for this commodity.

III. Personnel	1. Provide union information
	  a. Name
	  b. Current contract expiration date
	  c. Labor history over last 5 years
	    1. Strike dates
	    2. Strike durations
	2. Supply key-individual organization chart and backup personnel

IV. Quality & Testing Certifications	Check following capabilities that your facilities and personnel possesses:
	1. Certify to
	  a. ASTM
	  b. AWS
	  c. AISI
	  d. AMS Specs
	  e. ABS
	  f. Etc.
	2. Certification of material to military specs.
	3. Liquid-penetrant testing.
	4. Eddy-current testing.
	5. Magnetic-particle testing.
	6. Ultrasonic testing.
	7. Alloy-identify testing.
	8. Hydrostatic testing.
	9. Heat-treating capability.
	10. Impact-testing capacity.
	11. X-ray capability.
	12. Weld-repair qualifications.

V. Similar Products	Name other products that you have produced requiring similar capability as this commodity. Name companies for which these products were/are produced.

For _____ Commodity (Insert Name)

5. *Similar products*. Note similar products to prepare for in-plant inspection if the above considerations appear adequate.

As you can see, by using Form 16 and by applying the above analysis, you will be able either to set the stage for a meaningful plant visit in the event that the vendor appears qualified, or to dismiss the vendor without incurring this expense. Assuming that the vendor seems qualified, you should then schedule a plant visitation in conjunction with your quality and manufacturing personnel to audit against the statements in this form. You will also find it beneficial to maintain a master list of qualified vendors.

$\overline{\underline{=}}$Appendix 10

MATERIAL-REQUIREMENTS FORECASTING

It is difficult and costly to obtain precision in commodity-requirements forecasting, but, if you're willing to spend enough money, practically any degree of precision is possible. For instance, if the savings potential of material-forecast accuracy is great enough, you may find it desirable to restrict or slant your sales effort towards making a beneficial forecast come true.

However, before investing in a costly forecast, you should identify the value of different degrees of precision to discover if the investment is justified. In order to derive this value, an estimate of variation in expected usage is needed. The discussion below reviews two basic methods for obtaining this estimate and its application. This discussion is provided not to make you a forecasting expert, but instead to allow you to guide the efforts of others in providing you with a meaningful forecast. Which of the two techniques, the sales forecast method, or the shop load method, is the best for you will depend on your product mix, product leadtime, and reliability of sales forecast.

Each of these methods requires identification of the relationship of material usage to movements of the indicator (sales forecast or shop load). The sales forecast method is preferable if shop loads are not scheduled far in advance (e.g., short product leadtimes) and/or if your product is reasonably standardized in material usage. If shop loads are scheduled far in advance and your product has little standardized material usage, the shop load method would be preferred.

Both of these methods require historical information in order to develop relationships. The sales forecast technique requires knowledge of material usage as related to size or capacity within each sales class, as well as of scheduled shipment dates for above contracts related to material-use date. The shop load technique requires knowledge of material usage per shop per period under investigation, and also of man-hours scheduled per shop per period under investigation.

The objective of both techniques is to develop relationships that will enable compiling statistical material usage (magnitude and timing) with respect to forecasts of sales or shop load. Without getting into the details of various statistical techniques, correlation analysis is preferred for developing this type of relationship and generally would be applied as follows.

Sales Forecast Method

In applying the sales forecast method, you must identify those factors that will affect the amount of material used. In most cases, the significant factors will be sales class and size of the unit within the sales class.

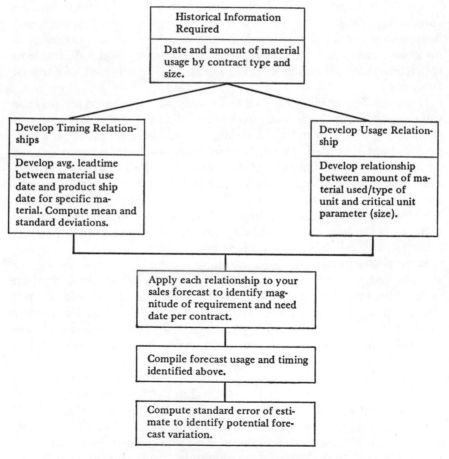

FIGURE 27.   Sales-Requirements Forecasting

FIGURE 28. Example Relationships

Commodity Description	Unit Type	Material Use Related To Unit Size (X)	Standard Error	Average Usage Related To Unit Ship Date	Standard Deviations
S.S. Plate, 1/2"	A	10 + .5 (X) Plates	± 20	- 3 Wks	± 1 Wk.
Weld Wire, 1/2"	B	180 + 25 (X) Pounds	± 50	- 6 Wks.	± 1.5 Wk.

Example Forecast

Description	Sales Forecast		Material Usage	Standard Error of Estimate	Forecast Timing	Favorable Req. Timing	Min.	Max.
	Unit Type	Unit Size						
S.S. Plate, 1/2"	A	1,000	$10 + (.5)$ $(1000) = 510$	$\pm \dfrac{20(3)}{\sqrt{3}}$	10/73	7/73	6/73	8/73
	A	2,000	$10 + (.5)$ $(2000) = 1010$		11/73	8/73	7/73	9/73
	A	1,500	$10 + (.5)$ $(1500) = 760$		12/73	9/73	8/73	10/73

Total 2nd Quarter = 2280 ± 34.6 Most Favorable
1010 + 20 Minimum

Then, using correlation analysis, which relates these factors to historical material usage, you can identify the expected material usage of each sales class and size in terms of the average and expected minimum and maximum deviation. The same type of approach is necessary to identify the expected need date for this material relative to the forecasted sales-contract shipping date. Through correlation analysis, you can identify the average leadtime and variation of need or shop use with respect to contract shipment schedules. Then, by merging these two relationships and combining them with the sales forecast you can derive your usage forecast. This approach is charted above along with sample relationships and their results when applied to the sales forecast.

Shop Loading Forecasting

The shop load approach to forecasting uses the same material that you have just reviewed. This shop load-material forecasting application is nearly identical to the sales forecasting method except that the material-use date did not require separate statistical analysis since it is explicit in the shop date. The shop load approach can be summarized as follows:

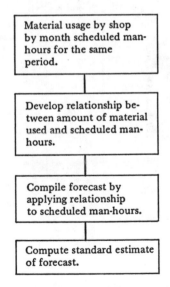

FIGURE 29.   Shop Load-Requirements Forecasting

The results in forecasting annual usage for steel in a job-shop production atmosphere were almost identical for the two techniques. However, as indicated in Chapter 4, due to the nature of the business in which these forecasts were generated (job shop: little standardization in material usage between similar units and long leadtimes from date of usage to ship date), the shop load method provided greater accuracy in the short run.

Summary

The key steps in each of these techniques can be summarized as follows:

1. Identify factors that result in changes in material usage.
2. Collect historical data on factors vs. usage.
3. Run correlation analysis to identify expected usage related to factors and anticipated accuracy.
4. Apply forecast of factors to relationship and compile usage estimate.
5. Compute standard error of forecast based on forecasted sample size and identified variance.

$\bar{\Xi}$Appendix 11

INFLATION FORECASTING

The primary use of escalation forecasting as discussed in this section has been to assist in establishing negotiation strategy concerning the value of price protection. As an illustration of this application, assuming that the curve in Figure 30 represents price movements for a commodity of interest, the value of a maximum escalation, firm price or an escalation-hedging provision in a contract is going to be quite different at point A than at point B. At point A, a term contract could actually prove detrimental unless you have also negotiated a deescalation clause; hedge buying, obviously, would be out of of the question. However, at point B the question is not whether you should engage in these activities, but what should you be willing to settle for in the way of maximum escalation, or of what value will a vendor's firm-price offering be compared to another's maximum-escalation offer?

Although the ability to make good purchasing decisions through inflation forecasting produces a significant advantage, the benefits of material-inflation forecasting are not confined to purchasing. Accurate inflation forecasts will also assist your controller in estimating his material cash flows to anticipate fund requirements and to insure that sufficient funds are available. An accurate forecast will enable your sales and estimating departments to sell products at acceptable prices and profitability levels. With purchased material accounting for 50 percent

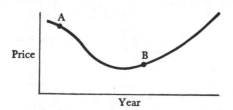

FIGURE 30.   Price Movements

211

of the sales dollar in many firms, inaccurate estimates of escalation could easily result in loss of sales or unprofitable operation.

Before describing a recommended approach to forecasting material prices, let us discuss briefly what you should expect from a forecast. First of all, a good forecast, contrary to what forecasters would like to have you believe, is rarely precise in its prediction. A good forecast usually is just less wrong than other forecast methods that could have been applied. But this expectation of imprecision does not negate the necessity for sound or close forecasts. Forecast closeness enables sounder decisions to be made in both negotiations and pricing, and that means profit to your company.

FORECASTING METHODS

There are many approaches currently used in industry to forecast material inflation. The two most widely used for material forecasting can be classified as trend and vendor techniques.

Trend Forecasting

Trend forecasting, projecting the historical price increase into the future, was a relatively sound technique for short-term forecasting in the early and middle 1960s, but has been totally inadequate for forecasting escalation in the period from 1968 through 1973. This is due to the assumption made in trend forecasting that the rate of escalation achieved historically will continue into the future. This assumption will be relatively valid in a period of constant legislative and administrative direction but didn't hold up with the differing emphases and circumstances of the Eisenhower, Kennedy, Johnson, and Nixon adminis-

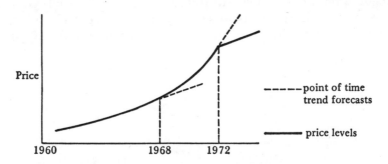

FIGURE 31.   Trend-Forecasting Deficiency

trations. Situations affecting escalation have altered drastically in the past few years and can be expected to continue to change. Since trend forecasting is not capable of identifying and anticipating the effect of these changes, this method is not reliable for accurate forecasting.

Vendor Forecasting

A seemingly logical method to overcome the weakness of trend forecasting and incur minimal expense would be to ask the vendor to provide forecasts. After all, who is closer to the market and has a greater stake in what happens? If anyone should be able to consider all potential variables and provide a sound forecast, the vendor should since he is staking his business future on pricing and capital strategies that are greatly influenced by potential market price and demand movements.

However, from a marketing position, the vendor is the least likely to provide an accurate forecast. Instead, he is most likely to provide an extremely conservative (high) forecast. This could be anticipated if you consider the consequences of the vendor providing a low forecast rather than one that is too high (again recognizing that precision is unexpected). If the forecast is too low, the vendor can lose through escalation clauses that don't provide adequate movement or through the realization that his price has escalated faster than anticipated, in which case the vendor's error and your resulting lost profit are readily seen and the potential for punitive action on your part is great.

If, on the other hand, the vendor estimates high, he can gain through a resulting escalation clause or he will look like a champion in being able to hold down your escalation. Your lost sales and overstated cost of goods sold that may have resulted from his estimates are extremely difficult to pinpoint and credit against his account. Consequently, the vendor has everything to gain through a high estimate and nothing to gain through a low estimate. In my own experience, in the face of an oversupplied market and reduced cost of production, when market forces could be almost certain to result in a price decrease, I have had vendors confidently predict recurrence of the same increase as in the previous year. This result is the rule rather than the exception.

If, as described above, the vendor has everything to gain from a high estimate, you have everything to lose and must search for an alternate technique that offers greater insight into future escalation.

Vendor Cost-Price Forecasting

A recommended forecasting technique that provides multiple benefits, especially for the larger corporation, is vendor cost-price forecasting. The intent of this section is not to convert buyers into forecasters. There are experts available either inside or outside your company to provide this necessary function. The intent, instead, is to enable a buyer to criticize a forecast, identify the type he should request, and use his trade publications to update existing forecasts. In conjunction with these objectives, a review of the basic methodology of this recommended forecast technique is in order.

Model Development

The first step in this method is to identify the major cost elements contributing to the price of the commodity and their relative cost contributions. In Figure 32, the cost elements and price contributions for a valve are identified.

Once these basic cost relationships have been determined, the next step is to apply this cost model to identify to what degree past prices have been influenced by movements in these cost elements, in order to discover the amount of cost versus supply/demand influence existent in your commodity. This analysis can be depicted as in Figure 33. You can identify the price levels through review of your history files and convert those prices to indexes. Cost levels can be determined by multiplying the cost indexes of labor and materials (identified in your relative contribution review) by the applicable contribution percentage, and totaling the

FIGURE 32.   Relative Contribution of Steel Valve–Elements

Elements	Contributions
1. Labor	50%
2. Steel Costing	
a. Steel	25%
b. Labor	15%
3. Miscellaneous	10%

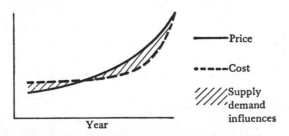

FIGURE 33.   Price-Supply-Cost Influence

result for each of the above years. Then, statistically through regressive-correlation analysis, you can identify the relationship of the cost-supply/demand effect to a production/capacity indicator. Once this identification is made, you will have derived a model that indicates:

$$Price = a + b_{x_1} + c_{x_2}$$

Where: a, b, c = Constants
x_1 = Element Costs
x_2 = Supply/Demand Indicator

Through application of this model and a forecast of element costs and the supply/demand indicator, you can forecast price. As an illustration of this process, if the model result was :

$$Price = .5 + .4\ (X_1) + .1\ (X_2)$$

and the X_1, X_2 forecasts were as in Table 12, the price forecast would be as in Table 13.

Cost Element Forecast

Obviously, the key to success in this forecast technique must be not only to develop an accurate model but also to generate accurate element forecasts for insertion in the model. You, in purchasing, will have difficulty in judging the adequacy of the model itself. You can, however, easily survey the cost-element forecasts to review where they may be

TABLE 12. Cost Element Forecast Results

	Year			
Forecast	1	2	3	4
X_1	1.10	1.15	1.20	1.30
X_2	1.02	1.30	0.90	1.10

TABLE 13. Price Forecast Results

Year	Forecast Equation	Price Forecast
1	$(.5 + .4(1.10) + .1\ (1.02)\ )$	1.042
2	$(.5 + .4(1.15) + .1\ (1.30)\ )$	1.090
3	$(.5 + .4(1.20) + .1\ (0.90)\ )$	1.070
4	$(.5 + .4(1.30) + .1\ (1.10)\ )$	1.130

diverging from actual cost movements in order to gain an early warning of a potentially troublesome forecast.

In Table 13, all the cost elements were grouped into one variable X_1. In order to forecast X_1, however, it is strongly suggested that your forecaster make individual forecasts of each of the cost elements (for the valve these were labor, steel, miscellaneous) and then develop this composite based on the relative weights (Labor = 65 percent, Steel = 25 percent, Miscellaneous = 10 percent).

In order to forecast these individual elements — steel, for instance — develop a primary cost breakdown on each until you get down to the level of basic elements (labor, ores, gases, etc.). Assume that your forecaster related inflation in these cost elements to an economic indicator (GNP, the wholesale-price index, or consumer price indexes are recommended) and a supply/demand indicator for that industry. For instance, one of the steel cost elements may be iron ore (pellets and/or scrap are often substituted) and past increases in the price of iron ore should then be related to GNP and supply/demand (see Figure 34).

Advantages of Cost-Price Forecasting

As is evident from this brief review, application of a technique of this type is much more time-consuming than either vendor or trend forecasting. For a small company or a lone division it would be extremely difficult to justify except on the few key or highest-cost commodity classes procured. However, for a large corporation, the technique is justifiable for a large percentage of the commodities procured. As in the example, if you forecast the basic raw materials such as steel, this forecast serves as a basic input to forecasts of many other finished goods prices. Once these basic forecasts are completed, any number of subforecasts can be spun off. In order to forecast prices for additional commodities from these basic commodity forecasts, you need only weigh the basic forecasts for the applicable relative costs and compile the re-

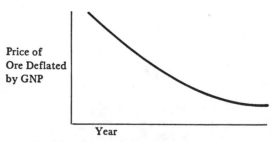

FIGURE 34.   Deflated-Element Forecast

sults. As an illustration of the sub-forecast available from forecasting a basic commodity, it is interesting to note the number of other cost elements you are forecasting in anticipating steel prices that influence your own production costs, as well as those of steel and other commodities. To name a few, you forecast prices of ores, natural gas, petroleum, electricity, coal, scrap, and oxygen.

This technique will be much more precise than the trend or vendor forecasting. In the first place, this technique forces the forecaster to explicitly state the assumptions he has made regarding cost movements and the influence of cost and supply and demand relationships. These assumptions are hidden in both trend and vendor forecasting. As stated before, forecasts are not expected to yield precision, but exposure of the assumptions reveals why the forecast erred; it can then be refined. In trend or vendor forecasting you are left with the hope that you will do better the next time.

Secondly, this technique allows you to call on experts whose business is predicting economic movements to supplement your forecast once you have developed the relationship described above. Unlike trend forecasting that simply assumes history will repeat itself, this technique allows you to use an expert's prediction of future economic activity. Further, with the increasing government influence experienced over the last ten years in the major industries, the magnitude of price rises will be increasingly sensitive to cost influences and cost influence is the primary concentration of this technique.

Finally, due to the existence of long-term labor contracts in more and more industries, in many cases crystal-ball gazing with respect to labor cost increases is necessary. The steel industry, for example, issues three-year contracts, and from the day of issuance you know what the magnitude of labor increases will be for the next three years. Again, by dealing with the cost elements you are able to separate certain from uncertain elements and concentrate on refining the degree of uncertainty.

Besides providing escalation/negotiation information for purchasing and pricing and cash flow forecasts for finance, the application of this technique has another major benefit. The golden rule of effective purchasing is "know your vendor." The more information you have available concerning his business, the better your position to effectively identify means of improving your material-related costs. A key element in value analysis, respecification, and make-or-buy application, is investigating higher cost areas in vendor manufacture to get a handle on the optimum improvement tactics to be applied. This method of forecasting provides that "handle" in the form of the estimated vendor-cost structure.

SUMMARY

In summary, the forecasting technique described in this section, vendor cost-price forecasting, offers many advantages in obtaining forecasting precision and information useful to other activities such as value analysis. However, due to the cost build-up approach, the expense required to apply this technique would probably be justified only for a relatively large corporation in which each individual cost element forecast could be used in many different ways.

Advantages discussed for this technique are:

1. Increased precision through
   a. stating cost price assumption
   b. experts supporting economic predictions
   c. using long-term labor contract information
   d. taking advantage of administrative cost-price control efforts by applying a cost-price forecast
2. Increased vendor knowledge useful for
   a. value analysis
   b. negotiations
3. Inflation forecasts for 10–15 basic commodities used in the production of steel will provide the cost information necessary to forecasting practically all major commodities (many of which are used in your own production as well as that of your vendor's)

Very briefly, application of this technique requires:

1. Determination of relative value of cost elements through research of:
   a. income, balance sheet statement
   b. supplier information
   c. engineering, industrial engineering estimates
   d. published information
2. Historical identification of relationship between cost elements, supply/demand, economic indicators, and price
3. A forecast of economic indicators
4. Combination of the indicator forecast with the relationship to derive price forecast

Index